MILITARY AND VETERAN ISSUES

THE POST-9/11 GI BILL

ADMINISTRATIVE ISSUES AND RECOMMENDATIONS

MILITARY AND VETERAN ISSUES

Additional books in this series can be found on Nova's website under the Series tab.

Additional e-books in this series can be found on Nova's website under eBooks tab.

MILITARY AND VETERAN ISSUES

THE POST-9/11 GI BILL

ADMINISTRATIVE ISSUES AND RECOMMENDATIONS

DELORES NORTON
EDITOR

NOVINKA
New York

NOTICE TO THE READER

Library of Congress Cataloging-in-Publication Data

ISBN: 978-1-63485-161-9

Published by Nova Science Publishers, Inc. † New York

Contents

PREFACE

This book compares and contrasts the administration of the Post-9/11 Veterans Educational Assistance Act of 2008 — enacted as Title V of the Supplemental Appropriations Act, 2008 — and Federal Pell Grants, as authorized by Title IV-A-1 of the Higher Education Act (HEA). The Post-9/11 GI Bill provides educational assistance payments to eligible servicemembers and veterans, and their dependents. One of its primary objectives is readjustment of veterans to civilian life and the workforce. The federal Pell Grant program provides grant aid payments to eligible and financially needy undergraduate students, regardless of military service record. One of its primary objectives is to increase postsecondary education access of low-income individuals. This book investigates whether the administrative processes supporting Pell Grants can provide lessons for achieving more timely, efficient, and student-friendly administration of the Post-9/11 GI Bill, thus ensuring that it achieves its policy objectives with respect to educational achievement of the target population. Furthermore, the book examines the extent of overpayments made in the Post-9/11 GI Bill; how effectively VA has addressed their causes; and the effectiveness of VA's collection efforts.

In: The Post-9/11 GI Bill
Editor: Delores Norton

ISBN: 978-1-63485-161-9

Chapter 1

COMPARISON OF POST-9/11 GI BILL® AND PELL GRANT ADMINISTRATION*

Cassandria Dortch

SUMMARY

This report compares and contrasts the administration of the Post-9/11 Veterans Educational Assistance Act of 2008 (Post-9/11 GI Bill®)—enacted as Title V of the Supplemental Appropriations Act, 2008 (P.L. 110-252)—and Federal Pell Grants, as authorized by Title IV-A-1 of the Higher Education Act (HEA). The Post-9/11 GI Bill provides educational assistance payments to eligible servicemembers and veterans, and their dependents. One of its primary objectives is readjustment of veterans to civilian life and the workforce. The federal Pell Grant program provides grant aid payments to eligible and financially needy undergraduate students, regardless of military service record. One of its primary objectives is to increase postsecondary education access of low-income individuals. The report investigates whether the administrative processes supporting Pell Grants can provide lessons for achieving more timely, efficient, and student-friendly administration of the Post-9/11 GI Bill, thus ensuring that it achieves its policy objectives with respect to educational achievement of the target population.

There are several differences between the programs and their administration. Post-9/11 GI Bill eligibility is contingent on service in the

* This is an edited, reformatted and augmented version of a Congressional Research Service, Publication No. R44088, dated June 24, 2015.

uniformed services, whereas Pell Grant eligibility is contingent on financial need. Post-9/11 GI Bill benefits must be used within several years of discharge from active duty, whereas Pell Grants can be used at any stage of an individual's life. The Post-9/11 GI Bill benefit was designed to meet most costs of education, whereas the Pell Grants were designed to meet a portion of an individual's financial need. Eligible individuals may receive both benefits concurrently.

When comparing the administrative processes of the programs, there are at least three important considerations. One is the difference in the number of beneficiaries/recipients—estimates indicate there were fewer than 1 million Post-9/11 GI Bill participants and more than 9 million Pell Grant recipients in FY2014, which leads to economies of scale and greater familiarity for Pell Grant administrators. Another is the greater variety of programs of education approved for the Post-9/11 GI Bill, which increases administrative complexity. Finally, while the Post-9/11 GI Bill went into effect in 2009, the Pell Grant administrative processes are more mature, having been developed and administered for decades.

There are areas in which the Post-9/11 GI Bill processes and procedures arguably could be improved if compared to the Pell Grant program. The key area would be a larger investment in system automation and internal controls to more fully automate the processes and maintain them with respect to ongoing legislative changes. For example, Post-9/11 GI Bill eligibility determinations could be more fully automated. VA systems could choose the most advantageous GI Bill programs based on applicant information. Exact payments and unmet costs may be estimated for Post-9/11 GI Bill participants prior to enrollment to encourage informed enrollment. Providing payments to educational institutions to disburse to students may eliminate an extra processing step by the VA and speed payments and adjustments. Overpayments of Post-9/11 GI Bill payments could be resolved through deductions from subsequent Post-9/11 GI Bill payments or other VA benefit payments.

However, there may be underlying issues that prevent or hinder improvements and may suggest a limited advantage from them. For example, a single lump sum housing allowance payment before the start or at the beginning of the academic term may help pay early housing expenses; however, it may increase the incidence and amount of overpayments and debts.

INTRODUCTION

The Post-9/11 Veterans Educational Assistance Act of 2008 (Post-9/11 GI Bill®)—enacted as Title V of the Supplemental Appropriations Act, 2008 (P.L. 110-252)[1]—provides educational assistance payments to eligible individuals (servicemembers and veterans, and their dependents) from the Department of Veterans Affairs (VA) in accordance with their military service. The Department of Education's (ED's) Federal Pell Grants, as authorized by Title IV-A-1 of the Higher Education Act (HEA), provide grant aid payments to eligible undergraduate students in accordance with their financial need, regardless of military service record. Timely, efficient, and student-friendly administration is important in ensuring that each federal program achieves its policy objectives with respect to the target population. Each program has developed administrative processes, systems, and procedures designed to streamline aid administration.

This report compares and contrasts administration of Post-9/11 GI Bill benefits and Pell Grant payments. Some participants have criticized the administration of Post-9/11 GI Bill payments for taking too long and asserted that the penalties for participants who received an overpayment of benefits are too high as compared to ED student aid programs. Some participant criticism is a result of simultaneous experience navigating the processes to receive Post-9/11 GI Bill benefits and Pell Grant payments. Since passage of the Post-9/11 GI Bill, the House Veterans' Affairs Committee has held several oversight hearings to ensure administration of the Post-9/11 GI Bill meets the needs of servicemembers transitioning to civilian life.[2] The hearings have focused on automation, timeliness of payments, and accuracy of benefits. Some of the differences in aid processing are a consequence of the programs' purposes. However, other differences in the processing design and operation may expose opportunities for improvement.

This report is designed to assist congressional staff seeking an exploration of ways in which the administration of Post-9/11 GI Bill benefits might be improved through the adoption of practices employed in the administration of Title IV aid. The report approaches this task through an examination of the statutory and regulatory provisions that are pertinent to the design and administration of Post-9/11 GI Bill benefits and Pell Grants, the Title IV aid program that is seemingly the most comparable to Post-9/11 GI Bill benefits. The report also examines the operational practices employed to implement statutory and regulatory provisions. Information on operational practices, particularly those relevant to aid administration, has been obtained through a review of sub-regulatory guidance materials, manuals providing guidance to staff involved in administering aid, and through a limited set of interviews and site visits with individuals at federal agencies and colleges who are directly involved in administering aid. The report presents a thorough description of the administrative practices used for each of these educational assistance programs and attempts to identify differences and reasons for differences in the administrative practices used across the programs. It also identifies some ways in which existing practices might be enhanced, and discusses possible ways Post-9/11 GI bill benefit administration might be improved by adopting some Title IV practices. It is hoped that this examination can help inform the dialogue on ways in which practices employed in the administration of one program may warrant consideration for their potential to streamline or enhance the administration of the other.

The report does not intend to compare benefit levels, evaluate the process and rationale for calculating benefit amounts, or contrast the processes for approving GI Bill programs of education and for determining institutional eligibility and eligible programs of education for the Pell Grant program.

Of the GI Bills administered by the VA and federal student aid programs administered by ED, the Post-9/11 GI Bill and Pell Grant programs were chosen for this analysis because of their commonalities. Neither program requires recipients to repay the funds, barring extenuating circumstances. Both programs are the largest educational assistance direct payment programs in terms of the numbers of participants and direct funding in each agency.

This report begins with a brief overview of the two programs and a table summarizing the key administrative activities and differences. Please note that the statutory authorizations and administrative processes are designed and implemented independently without any required intersection. Subsequent sections of the report provide an in-depth explanation of the administrative activities from the application process to the calculation of benefits to the disbursement of funds and the process for participants and educational institutions to resolve GI Bill payments that exceeded a participant's eligibility (overpayments). The final section highlights associated and articulated issues and concerns about the administrative processes to explicate opportunities for improvement in each. For assistance with frequently used acronyms, see Appendix B.

OVERVIEW OF PROGRAMS

This section provides a brief overview of program aspects that are helpful in understanding key similarities and differences in their administration. While the Post-9/11 GI Bill and Pell Grant programs are mutually exclusive, an individual may receive benefits from both programs concurrently if the individual is eligible for both programs independently.

Post-9/11 GI Bill

The federal government supports the readjustment of veterans through continued education and training, principally through programs authorized under Title 38 and Title 10 of the U.S. Code. The programs, known as GI Bills, offer educational assistance through monetary payments to veterans and servicemembers, and their family members. The active GI Bills are the Post-9/11 GI Bill, Montgomery GI Bill-Active Duty (MGIB-AD), the Survivors' and Dependents' Educational Assistance Program (DEA), the Montgomery GI Bill-Selected Reserve (MGIB-SR), the Reserve Educational Assistance Program (REAP), and the Post-Vietnam Era Veterans Educational Assistance Program (VEAP).[3] In FY2014, about $12 billion in GI Bill benefits were paid on behalf of approximately 1 million individuals.[4]

The Post-9/11 GI Bill (Title 38 U.S.C., Chapter 33) is intended to support qualifying individuals who served on active duty in the uniformed services on or after September 10, 2001, in their readjustment to civilian life, and to support retention in the uniformed services.[5] Qualifying individuals may receive educational assistance payments while enrolled in approved programs of education or training. Approved programs include, but are not limited to, secondary school, non-college degree programs (NCD), postsecondary degree programs, vocational flight training, correspondence programs, apprenticeship or on-the-job training, and licensure, certification, and academic tests.[6] The programs may be outside the United States.

Dependents of qualifying individuals who are pursuing an approved program of education may also be eligible for Post-9/11 GI Bill benefits. Dependents may receive a transfer of entitlement (ToE) from a qualifying individual or may receive entitlement (Marine Gunnery Sergeant John David Fry Scholarship Program, Fry Scholarship) as a result of a qualifying individual's death in the line of duty while on active duty on or after September 11, 2001.

Program benefit levels were originally designed to reward individuals for their service during a time of arduous conflict by covering the full cost of public undergraduate education for in-state students.[7] Eligible individuals may receive one or more of the following payments: tuition and fees, Yellow Ribbon GI Education Enhancement Program Payments (YR payments),[8] housing allowance, books and supplies stipend, tutorial assistance, licensing and certification test fees, national test fees, relocation and travel assistance, supplemental assistance, and Tuition Assistance “Top Up” payments. Statutory provisions establish maximum amounts for most of the payments. Individuals may receive less than the maximum for a variety of reasons, including, but not limited to, the eligible individual’s type of enrollment or pursuit, rate of enrollment or pursuit, active duty status, and aggregate length of qualifying active duty service.

Eligible individuals are entitled to 36 months (or the part-time equivalent) of Post-9/11 GI Bill benefits, which must be used within a period specified in statute. Entitlement is charged one day for one day of full-time pursuit, a proportional percentage of a day for less-than-full-time pursuit, or one day depending on the amount of the payment. The period during which entitlement may be used depends on the qualifying individual’s length of service, and either the qualifying individual’s date of discharge or release from active duty or the child’s age or receipt of a high school diploma or the equivalent.[9]

Individuals apply to the VA for benefits, and it certifies their eligibility. Once an individual’s educational institution or training establishment certifies enrollment or pursuit of an approved program of education, the VA pays benefits to the individual and institution, as appropriate.

Over three-quarters of a million individuals received over $10 billion in Post-9/11 GI Bill benefits in FY2013.[10] In academic year 2012-2013, there were, on average, 73 Post-9/11 GI Bill participants at each educational institution that had at least one. Approximately 14% of institutions with a Post-9/11 GI Bill participant enrolled only one recipient, and approximately 16% enrolled 100 or more recipients.[11]

Educational institutions and training establishments receive a reporting fee of $12 per GI Bill and Vocational Rehabilitation and Employment program (VR&E) participant and $15 per GI Bill and VR&E participant that receives an advanced payment.[12] The fee may be used to support the costs of certification or programs for veterans. The VA paid over $10 million in reporting fees in FY2013, in addition to participant benefits.

Federal Pell Grant Program

The federal government supports access to postsecondary education, primarily through programs authorized by the Higher Education Act (HEA). Title IV of the HEA authorizes a broad array of federal student aid programs that assist students and their families with paying for or financing the costs of obtaining a postsecondary education. The programs include Pell Grants, Stafford Loans, Federal Supplemental Educational Opportunity Grants (FSEOG), the Teacher Education Assistance for College and Higher Education (TEACH) Grant program, Federal Perkins Loans, and Federal Work-Study programs.[13] In FY2014, nearly $134 billion in HEA Title IV aid was made available to almost 13 million students.[14]

The Federal Pell Grant program, the single largest source of federal grant aid supporting postsecondary students, is intended to increase access to postsecondary education for financially needy individuals. Eligible individuals may receive a grant of money while enrolled in eligible programs at an eligible institution of higher education (IHE; see **Appendix A** for a description of an IHE). The benefits were originally designed to help qualified high school graduates with exceptional financial need take advantage of the benefits of higher education.[15] Pell Grants are intended to be the foundation for all federal student aid.

To be eligible for a Pell Grant in award year[16] 2014-2015, students must meet several criteria: completion of secondary school or an equivalent,[17] citizenship or eligible noncitizen status,[18] Selective Service registration,[19] and pursuit of an eligible program at an eligible institution. Several situations related to a drug conviction, other Title IV aid (e.g., defaulting on student loans), and institutionalization may disqualify otherwise eligible individuals from receiving a Pell Grant.[20]

Pell Grant funds are available to students enrolled for the purpose of earning a certificate or degree in an eligible program at a domestic, Title IV-participating IHE.[21] Given statutory and regulatory criteria,[22] eligible programs may be undergraduate courses of study; post-baccalaureate K-12 teacher certification or licensure programs if enrolled at least half-time; one year of noncredit or reduced-credit remedial coursework;[23] correspondence programs;[24] flight school programs; English as a second language (ESL) courses; cooperative education programs; and for students with an intellectual disability, as defined in the HEA, a comprehensive transition and postsecondary program for students with intellectual disabilities.

Cumulative lifetime eligibility for Pell Grant aid is limited to six awards or 12 full-time semesters (or the equivalent) for all recipients. During each award year, eligible individuals may receive up to a maximum amount ($5,730 in award year 2014-2015) determined by statutory provisions. The amount may be reduced depending on the financial need of the student and his/her family, the student's educational expenses, and the student's enrollment status.

Individuals apply for a Pell Grant by filling out the Free Application for Federal Student Aid (FAFSA®[25]). ED information technology systems process the FAFSA to determine the individual's basic eligibility and expected family contribution (EFC). The financial aid administrator at an IHE calculates the Pell Grant amount and awards it to the student's school account.

The program is estimated to have provided over $35.7 billion to approximately 9.7 million undergraduate students in FY2011. In award year 2011-2012, approximately 41% of all undergraduates in Title IV-participating IHEs were estimated to have received Pell Grants. Of those IHEs with Pell Grant recipients, there were, on average, over 1,000 Pell Grant recipients at each one. Approximately 15% of IHEs with Pell Grant recipients had fewer than 60.[26]

The Pell Grant program pays participating institutions an administrative cost allowance of $5 per enrolled recipient. This allowance is expected to offset some of the administrative costs of the Pell Grant program and other smaller Title IV aid programs.

KEY DIFFERENCES

There are several differences in the administration of the Post-9/11 GI Bill and Pell Grant programs. Table 2 provides a succinct overview of some key differences. A full explanation of each is available in the appropriate section following the table.

Some of the administrative differences may be a consequence of the relatively younger age of the Post-9/11 GI Bill; what may arguably be termed greater benefit complexity for the Post-9/11 GI Bill; and the complexity of DOD records. Because the Post-9/11 GI Bill was enacted in 2009 and the Pell Grant program was enacted in 1973, ED, IHEs, and Congress have had more time and resources to develop a suite of fully automated and integrated information systems, which administer Pell Grants in concert with the other HEA Title IV aid programs, and to improve process and system efficiency through administrative, regulatory, and legislative enhancements.[27] And although the VA has administered several GI Bill programs since 1944, the Post-9/11 GI Bill benefit architecture was not compatible with the legacy GI Bill information systems. Pell Grants are a single payment type intended to cover educational costs; while the most common Post-9/11 GI Bill benefit includes four different payments (tuition and fees, YR, housing, and books) intended to cover different educational costs and thus requiring differing award rules. Besides the most common Post-9/11 GI Bill payments, there are additional payment types covering less commonly utilized educational costs that require different information for certification and payment.

Differences in the level of automation are crucial to processing speed and accuracy. Finally while ED checks several Pell Grant eligibility criteria through automated database matching programs with other federal agencies, VA has been unable to fully automate the calculation of qualifying active duty service.[28] As a consequence, initial FAFSA processing is automated, but initial processing of applications for veterans education benefits is primarily manual. It may be of note that despite initial FAFSA automation, at least one data element on the application of almost half of all eligible applicants is verified manually by an FAA to ensure system integrity.[29]

Both programs allow individuals to apply online. The Post-9/11 GI Bill application requires most applicants to choose the most advantageous GI Bill. The Pell Grant application requires more information, including personal financial information, that confuses some applicants. A veteran may apply for and receive a certificate of eligibility for Post-9/11 GI Bill benefits at any time within their entitlement period even if he or she does not plan to use the benefits in the immediate future. A Pell Grant application is only processed for eligibility during college admissions or while attending college.

The initial benefit application is processed to determine eligibility. With respect to the Post-9/11 GI Bill, the VA cross references DOD data and several legacy systems and issues a certificate of eligibility (COE) to the individual within approximately 20 days.[30] The COE summarizes the individual's qualifying service and resulting benefit level (40%-100%), remaining entitlement, and delimiting date (the last date of eligibility for education benefits). With respect to Pell Grants, ED's Central Processing System (CPS)[31] automatically verifies basic eligibility for HEA Title IV aid, not necessarily the Pell Grant program in particular, by matching data from several federal agency databases. Within 3-5 days, CPS provides the applicant with a student aid report (SAR) that summarizes the application data and data match results, indicates the applicant's expected family contribution (EFC) and resulting potential Pell Grant amount, and provides additional HEA Title IV aid information for the application academic year.

After the initial application process, the VA and educational institutions share processing responsibility for Post-9/11 GI Bill benefits, whereas the remaining Pell Grant processes are primarily the responsibility of the IHEs. This difference may contribute to the differences in the time required to pay benefits and concerns regarding who is responsible for Post-9/11 GI Bill overpayments—the participant or educational institution. An overpayment occurs when a benefit amount is paid on behalf of a Post-9/11 GI Bill participant to the participant or to the educational institution, and then it is subsequently determined that the individual is eligible for a smaller amount.

Secondary claim/application processing determines benefit payment amounts based on actual or planned enrollment. An IHE may complete secondary processing in order to inform prospective students of their HEA Title IV aid package and encourage enrollment. The VA completes secondary processing only to award payments. For registered or enrolled students, the educational institution reports enrollment to the VA in order for the VA to calculate and make Post-9/11 GI Bill payments accordingly. The federal government encourages educational institutions to counsel GI Bill participants on the complexities of higher education and financial aid. For registered or enrolled students, the IHE may in special circumstances adjust some data elements used in calculating the HEA Title IV aid package, including Pell Grant payments, and make payments accordingly. The IHE reports Pell Grant payments to ED for payment.

The key differences between the handling of overpayments from the Post-9/11 GI Bill and Pell Grant programs have to do with the total amount of the overpayment and the related programs. A Pell Grant overpayment occurs when a student receives more aid than that which he or she is eligible. A single Post-9/11 GI Bill payment may exceed $20,000. A single Pell Grant disbursement in FY2014 was no more than $2,865. For purposes of Post-9/11 GI Bill payments, VA first sends debt notification letters to the participant explaining how the participant may choose to resolve the debt, before VA notifies credit reporting agencies and refers the debt to the Department of the Treasury. For purposes of Pell Grants, the FAA will first adjust a student's Title IV aid package during the current award year to eliminate an overpayment and then attempt to recoup the funds from the student before referring the debt to ED's Debt Resolution Services. The onus is primarily on the participant for Post-9/11 GI Bill purposes and on the IHE for Pell Grant purposes.

Table 1. Key Program and Administrative Differences: Post-9/11 GI Bill (Ch. 33) and Pell Grant Program (Additional criteria and qualifications may apply)

Area	Post-9/11 GI Bill (Ch. 33)	Pell Grant Program (Pell)	Key Differences
Purpose			
Policy Objectives	Reward military service, support readjustment to civilian life, ensure comprehensive educational benefits, and improve Armed Forces recruitment and retention.	Increase access to postsecondary education for individuals from low-income families, and serve as the foundational aid for needy undergraduates.	Ch. 33 serves uniformed servicemembers and their families; Pell serves individuals from low-income families. Ch. 33 rewards and promotes service in the uniformed services; Pell attempts to partially redress economic circumstance.
Program Characteristics/Components			
Eligible Individuals	Eligible servicemembers and veterans, and their eligible dependents.	Eligible undergraduates demonstrating financial need.	Ch. 33 eligibility primarily contingent on service in the uniformed services; Pell eligibility primarily contingent on financial need. Dependents of a qualifying individual may be eligible for Ch. 33. Pell eligibility cannot be transferred.

Table 1. (Continued)

Area	Post-9/11 GI Bill (Ch. 33)	Pell Grant Program (Pell)	Key Differences
Benefit Availability	Up to 36 months of full-time attendance/pursuit within 15 years of discharge (or within specified age range for dependent children).	Six full-time awards or 12 full-time semesters after high school completion or equivalent.	Ch. 33 provides the equivalent of four years of traditional college; Pell provides the equivalent of six years of traditional undergraduate education.a Ch. 33 entitlement expires over time; Pell eligibility does not.
Programs of Education	High school, vocational training, undergraduate and graduate postsecondary programs, flight training, apprenticeship, on-the-job training, licensure and certification, national tests.	Undergraduate programs and post-baccalaureate K-12 teacher certification programs that do not lead to graduate degrees and that are offered by institutions that do not offer a baccalaureate degree in education.	Ch. 33 benefits may be used for many programs of education and training; Pell is limited to traditional undergraduate education.a Ch. 33 benefits may be received for enrollment in foreign educational institutions; Pell may not.
Estimated FY2015 Participation and Costb	0.9 million individuals $12.4 billion	8.9 million individuals $33.9 billion	Pell pays benefits to about 10 times as many individuals as Ch. 33, but the average estimated FY2015 individual benefit amount for Pell ($3,826) is one-quarter that of Ch. 33 ($14,570).

Area	Post-9/11 GI Bill (Ch. 33)	Pell Grant Program (Pell)	Key Differences
Maximum Individual Benefit Level per Participant/Student	Tuition and fees charged, subject to caps; local housing costs;[c] $1,000 annual books and supplies stipend; $1,200 tutorial assistance; and $500 relocation and travel assistance.	Specified in statutory provisions (estimated $5,830 in award year 2015-2016), but not more than "cost of attendance."[d]	Ch. 33 covers education-related costs up to statutory limits; Pell covers education-related costs adjusted for the student's and family's assessed ability to pay, and up to the statutory limit.
Administration			
Administrator	The VA is primary administrator.	ED primarily pays contractors and schools to administer program.	The VA is the primary Ch. 33 administrator; contractors and schools are the primary Pell administrators.
Application	Veterans' Online Application (VONAPP) or paper VA Forms 22-1990, 22-1990e, or 22-5490.	Free Application for Federal Student Aid (FAFSA) completed online, on paper, through a toll-free number, or by financial aid administrator (FAA).	The estimated time required to complete each application is 15 minutes for VA Form 22-1990 and three hours for the FAFSA. The GI Bill benefit application must be completed by the applicant; the FAFSA may be completed by the applicant or by the FAA.

Table 1. (Continued)

Area	Post-9/11 GI Bill (Ch. 33)	Pell Grant Program (Pell)	Key Differences
			The GI Bill benefit application may be submitted within one year of enrollment; the FAFSA must be submitted by the end of the award year. Both applications are generally submitted prior to enrollment. GI Bill applicant must choose a GI Bill; FAFSA is a general application for HEA Title IV aid.
Initial Claim/Application Processing	The VA verifies DOD records, reviews prior GI Bill usage, determines eligibility, and issues Certificate of Eligibility (COE).	ED system checks against several federal databases, checks HEA Title IV aid history, determines basic eligibility, calculates expected family contribution (EFC), and produces student aid report (SAR) and institutional student information record (ISIR).	An original GI Bill claim is processed within 20 days, on average; FAFSA online is processed within 3-5 days. The VA primarily verifies DOD records manually; ED systems automatically verify records against the databases of several federal agencies, and then FAAs manually verify some data to improve system integrity.

Area	Post-9/11 GI Bill (Ch. 33)	Pell Grant Program (Pell)	Key Differences
			An original GI Bill claim is processed in multiple systems with multiple redundant data entry points; FAFSA is processed by a central processor in Iowa. Ch. 33 eligibility is determined by the VA; Pell Grant eligibility is determined by ED and FAAs. Veteran application processing at regional processing offices (RPOs) is subject to local conditions (e.g., weather); FAFSA processing is more independent of local conditions because it is automated. The COE is mailed; the SAR is available online for individuals who applied electronically.

Table 1. (Continued)

Area	Post-9/11 GI Bill (Ch. 33)	Pell Grant Program (Pell)	Key Differences
			The VA develops and implements the IT systems used to administer; ED and various third parties develop and implement IT systems.
Secondary Claim/Application Processing	The VA completes secondary processing based on certifications of enrollment or pursuit submitted by either the institution or individual.	The FAA packages aid and provides award letter to student.	Educational institution or training establishment certifies enrollment or pursuit before the VA makes Ch. 33 payments; IHE verifies enrollment to process or disburse Pell award. Ch. 33 benefits are only calculated for participants pursuing a program of education; a Pell Grant and Title IV aid package may be estimated for prospective students.

Area	Post-9/11 GI Bill (Ch. 33)	Pell Grant Program (Pell)	Key Differences
			Ch. 33 supports education and training with multiple types of payments; Pell supports traditional undergraduate education with one type of payment.a The VA maintains the list of approved programs of education for Ch. 33; for Pell, ED maintains the list of Title IV-eligible institutions, and the institutions maintain the list of eligible programs. The veterans claim examiner (VCE) may not take into consideration special circumstances of individuals for Ch. 33; the FAA may use professional judgment to adjust for special circu nstances of individuals affe ing the Pell award.

Table 1. (Continued)

Area	Post-9/11 GI Bill (Ch. 33)	Pell Grant Program (Pell)	Key Differences
			The VA makes educational and vocational counseling available to Ch. 33 participants. Educational institutions are encouraged to provide academic and financial advice to Ch. 33 participants; the VA and ED make college planning and financial aid information available. Ch. 33 payment amount calculations are explained to students; Pell amount calculations are less transparent.
Initial Payment Processing	The VA initiates payments to individuals and institutions, as applicable, and issues award letters.	Individual accepts aid package. The FAA disburses payments per schedule.	Ch. 33 tuition and fees payments for participants' enrollment at private educational institutions may vary significantly between academic terms

Area	Post-9/11 GI Bill (Ch. 33)	Pell Grant Program (Pell)	Key Differences
			because maximum amounts are paid until the annual maximum is met; Pell payments are generally the same for the fall and spring of a standard academic trimester academic year. The Ch. 33 housing allowance is available for every day eligible individuals are enrolled; a Pell award is not available for the final term of a standard term academic year (e.g., summer semester) for full-time students. With the exception of tuition and fees, Ch. 33 benefits (e.g., housing allowance) are paid for training and education completed; Pell awards are for education while it is being pursued.

Table 1. (Continued)

Area	Post-9/11 GI Bill (Ch. 33)	Pell Grant Program (Pell)	Key Differences
			VA makes Ch. 33 payments to participants and schools; IHEs disburse Pell payments to students' school accounts, IHE funds are reimbursed by ED. Some Ch. 33 payments are executed through a manual, paper process; Pell payments are primarily automated.
Subsequent/Ongoing Payments	School certifying officials (SCOs) correct or revise a previous certificate of enrollment if the participant's rate of pursuit changes or other factors change. SCOs and individuals must certify enrollment every academic term, month, year, or program, depending on the	For subsequent payments in the same award year, the student exhibits satisfactory academic progress, and the FAA disburses payments per schedule. For subsequent award years, the student resubmits FAFSA, and ED and the FAA reinitiate the processes starting with eligibility.	Ch. 33 participants do not reapply for subsequent benefits; Pell recipients must reapply annually. A change in enrollment mid-term may result in an overpayment due from the Ch. 33 participant to the VA or an adjustment of Pell funds in the subsequent term by the FAA.

Area	Post-9/11 GI Bill (Ch. 33)	Pell Grant Program (Pell)	Key Differences
	type of education and training, and completion of pursuit.		For the GI Bills, educational institutions define satisfactory academic progress; for HEA Title IV aid, IHEs define satisfactory academic progress according to minimum federal standards.
Payment Adjustments	SCO must report changes in VA-ONCE or submit VA Forms to VA.	FAA repackages HEA Title IV aid and may reduce subsequent Pell Grant award to ensure overpayments are eliminated.	VA assigns responsibility for resolving GI Bill issues either to participants or educational institutions; The FAAs are responsible for resolving issues with ED unless the student has an issue with the FAA.
Overpayments	Amount is calculated by the VA based on VA-ONCE. The VA issues debt letter to institution or individual. Institution or individual must repay debt, enter into payment plan, or appeal debt with VA Debt Management Center (DMC). Treasury Offset Program resolves long outstanding debts.	The IHE repays its overpayments to ED. The individual repays overpayments to the IHE. Unresolved individual debts are escalated by the IHE to ED's Debt Resolution Services, and while unresolved the individual loses HEA Title IV aid eligibility.	Ch. 33 overpayments must be resolved by the participant or school; most Pell Grant overpayments are resolved by the FAA adjusting other aid in the aid package in the same or subsequent payment period.

Source: Compiled by CRS based on a review of U.S. Code; Department of Veterans Affairs, School Certifying Official Handbook; Department of Veterans Affairs, VA-ONCE Guide; Department of Education, Student Aid Handbook; and other agency publications and documents.

[a] Traditional undergraduate education means undergraduate programs and institutions that are eligible for Title IV aid, as authorized by the Higher Education Act.

[b] FY2015 President's Budget Request.

[c] "Local housing costs" are determined by the Department of Defense for a member of the Armed Forces with dependents in pay grade E-5, and based on a survey of civilian housing costs for particular geographic locations.

[d] "Cost of attendance" is determined by the IHE based on an estimate of the full-time, full-year costs for a student, and generally including (depending on the circumstances) tuition and fees, books, supplies, transportation, miscellaneous personal expenses, room and board, dependent care, a first professional license or certificate, study-abroad, employment costs, and other costs defined in statutory provisions.

[e] Standard terms are semesters, trimesters, or quarters, as these words are traditionally used. In traditional usage, an individual semester or trimester provides about 14 to 17 weeks of instructional time and full-time is defined as at least 12 semester or trimester hours. The program's academic calendar generally consists of three terms, one each in fall, spring, and summer. In traditional usage of the term "quarter," an individual quarter provides about 10 to 12 weeks of instructional time, and full-time is defined as at least 12 quarter hours. The program's academic calendar generally includes three quarters in the fall, winter, and spring and often a summer quarter as well.

One difference key to every process step is the greater transparency in the Post-9/11 GI Bill program from the perspective of the participant. Many veterans may with little assistance correctly assess their Post-9/11 GI Bill eligibility and the payment amounts that they may receive. The eligibility criteria and calculations for Pell Grants would be difficult for students to duplicate accurately. For example, the key criterion for Post-9/11 GI Bill eligibility is the individual's service record, which may be obtained from their service unit if the exact dates are not remembered. A key criterion for Pell Grant eligibility is EFC, which is based on calculations using financial information, benefit receipt, and statutory provisions.

Benefit Application and Submission

The first step in benefit administration is notification from the individual of a desire to take advantage of a benefit. Individuals must apply for the Post-9/11 GI Bill and Pell Grant programs.

Application for Veterans Education Benefits

Eligible individuals apply for most GI Bill benefits, including Post-9/11 GI Bill benefits, by mail or by completing the Veteran's Online Application (VONAPP). There are separate paper forms for qualifying individuals, Fry scholarship beneficiaries, and transferees.[32] VONAPP allows servicemembers and veterans, and their families, to apply for various VA benefits, including, but not limited to, education, burial, or pension benefits. The application may be submitted as soon as the individual becomes eligible for the Post-9/11 GI Bill and must be submitted within one year of enrollment or the pursuit for which the individual would like payment.[33] The VA provides multiple modes of assistance to individuals completing the application and guarantees that it will respond to emailed questions within five to seven working days.

The application form requests the applicant's identifying information (e.g., Social Security number) and other information that assures the VA can contact the individual, make payments to the individual, and determine eligibility (e.g., service record). For dependents, the application also requires identifying information for the qualifying individual; and for Fry scholarship applicants, it requires a record of other VA benefits that the applicant has applied for or received.[34]

In addition, individuals must choose the education benefit program from which they would like to receive benefits. Qualifying individuals who are applying for Post-9/11 GI Bill benefits and who are eligible for at least one of the MGIB-AD, MGIB-SR, or REAP programs must make and date an irrevocable election to receive Post-9/11 GI Bill benefits in lieu of *one* of the aforementioned programs.[35]

The application notifies individuals that application processing may be expedited by sending proof of their service record and evidence of eligibility for supplemental benefits.

Once the application has been submitted, applicants may follow their application and benefit information through eBenefits. eBenefits is a portal for veterans, servicemembers, and their families to research, find, access, and eventually manage their benefits, as well as manage their personal information.

Pell Grant Application: FAFSA

The Free Application for Federal Student Aid (FAFSA) is the method for applying for a Pell Grant, other forms of HEA Title IV aid, and, in some instances, aid offered by states and IHEs. Most commonly, students complete and submit the FAFSA online; however, students may also submit the FAFSA by mail. Alternatively, schools may complete the FAFSA on behalf of students through the FAA Access to Central Processing System (CPS) Online portal. The FAFSA may be submitted as early as the January preceding the award year for which the individual would like aid, and it must be submitted before the end of the same award year (June 30). ED provides multiple modes of assistance to individuals completing the FAFSA, and many educational institutions, including high schools and nonprofit organizations, offer assistance.

There are over 100 questions on the FAFSA, but most applicants are not required to respond to all of them. The online form, FAFSA on the Web (FOTW), uses skip logic to present questions based on prior responses. For example, once a student identifies as female, the questions regarding registration for the draft are not posed because only males are required to register. As of February 2015, students complete FOTW in 20 minutes, on average.[36]

The FAFSA requests two types of information—identity and financial. The identity information includes contact information, information used to determine eligibility for HEA Title IV aid, data used to award state aid, and up to 13 questions to determine dependency status. Identity information is required for the applicant and, as applicable, a spouse and/or parents. In addition, applicants are prompted to list the schools that they want to receive their FAFSA information and to indicate interest in work-study. Financial information is also required for the applicant and, as applicable, a spouse and/or parents. This includes federal income tax return status and information, earnings and income, assets, child support, payments to savings plans, living allowances received, and veterans' noneducation benefits. The online form allows applicants to permit the system to retrieve the federal income tax form data directly from the Internal Revenue Service (IRS) and their tax return(s) through the IRS Data Retrieval Tool.

INITIAL CLAIM AND APPLICATION PROCESSING

The veteran's application for benefits and the FAFSA must be processed to verify the applicant's eligibility.

Post-9/11 GI Bill

GI Bill applications, also known as original claims, are processed at one of the four VA Regional Processing Offices (RPOs). Claims are routed to RPOs depending on either the address of the educational institution or training establishment or the address of the applicant. The capability to process a claim that has been routed to one RPO at another RPO is limited until the claimant's electronic file has been transferred to preserve claims management integrity.[37]

Eligibility Verification

The original claim (application for VA education benefits) is processed by the VA Veterans Claims Examiner (VCE) using several IT systems (**Table 3**). The VA has several legacy systems that are used to administer the other GI Bills and veterans benefits more generally. The VA developed the Long Term Solution (LTS) to automate processing of Post-9/11 GI Bill claims; however, LTS must work within the legacy system architecture.

Claim information is entered into The Image Management System (TIMS) for VCE review. The VCE is responsible for verifying the claimant's eligibility and either issuing a certificate of eligibility (COE) or issuing a letter explaining why the claimant is not currently eligible.

The first verification check reviews DOD records. The primary source is the Veterans Affairs/Department of Defense Identity Repository (VADIR). VADIR interfaces with LTS, which makes an initial eligibility determination; however, the VCE is often called upon to do additional research of missing information. The VCE may verify the service record and DOD education-related service obligations or benefits in the Veterans Information Solution (VIS), on a copy of the DD-214, on a copy of the Kicker contract, in the Beneficiary Identification and Record Locator Subsystem (BIRLS), or through contacting DOD or the service branch. The LTS calculates the aggregate period of qualifying service. For dependents, the VCE reviews records of the qualifying individual, the dependent, and, if applicable, the transfer of entitlement (ToE). VIS contains dependency and ToE data.

Table 2. Department of Veterans Affairs Education Related IT Systems

Acronym	System Title	Description
BIRLS	Beneficiary Identification and Record Locator Subsystem	A computerized record system containing basic identifying information on a VA claimant including current location of the claimant's folder and service information.
BDN	Benefits Delivery Network	A processing and payment system for all awards and related actions. It generates payment information that is sent to the Treasury for producing benefit checks. It also contains the master record files for VA beneficiaries.
LTS	Long Term Solution	A system for calculating Post-9/11 GI Bill eligibility, award amounts, and generating letters. It includes fully automated processing for many claims. Transactions are sent from LTS to BDN for payment.
PCGL	Personal Computer Generated Letters system	A computer system for generating letters that cannot be generated by the primary system, such as LTS or BDN.

Acronym	System Title	Description
TIMS	The Image Management System	An electronic folder management system.
VA-ONCE	VA-Online Certification of Enrollment	A VA Internet-based application used by educational institutions to certify student enrollment and submit notices of change in student status for VA education benefits.
VADIR	Veterans Affairs/Department of Defense Identity Repository	An electronic repository of military personnel's military history, payroll information, and their dependents' data provided to VA by DOD.a
VIS	Veterans Information Solution	An Intranet-based application that provides a consolidated read-only view of a subset of data gathered real-time from BIRLS, VADIR, BDN, and the Rating Board Automation (RBA2000) corporate database, which documents disability ratings.b
VONAPP	Veteran's Online Application	Allows servicemembers and veterans, and their families, to apply for various VA benefits, including, but not limited to, education, burial, or pension benefits.
WEAMS	Web Enabled Approval Management System	A database that stores information on the programs of education approved for GI Bill purposes.

Source: Compiled by CRS from various VA documents.

[a] Department of Veteran Affairs, "Notice of establishment of new system of records," 74 *Federal Register* 37093-37096, July 27, 2009.

[b] Department of Veteran Affairs (VA), "Notice of establishment of new system of records," 74 *Federal Register* 37309-37312, July 28, 2009.

The VCE reviews the Benefits Delivery Network (BDN) for usage of other GI Bills that may affect Post-9/11 GI Bill entitlement, verifies that the individual properly made an irrevocable election if required, validates the bank deposit routing number in BDN, updates the individual's contact information in BDN if applicable, and notes in TIMS whether the individual made the $1,200 contribution for MGIB-AD benefits. In addition, if the information is available the VCE may review whether the individual is eligible to pursue his/her desired program of education. The program of education review is also conducted as part of the secondary processing step discussed in the next section.

To facilitate future process audits and avoid duplicative efforts, the VCE captures and records in TIMS the sources and data used to confirm eligibility/ineligibility along with helpful notes.

If a claimant is ineligible for Post-9/11 GI Bill benefits, LTS generates a letter explaining the reason(s), evidence, and next steps. If needed, letters may also be prepared and customized using the Personal Computer Generated Letters (PCGL) system and then mailed manually. Denied claimants must work directly with the RPO to correct and resolve any issues.

Certificate of Eligibility (COE)

If the claimant's eligibility for Post-9/11 GI Bill benefits is verified, LTS generates a COE. In order to prepare the COE, the VCE must ensure LTS is appropriately and accurately populated. Although LTS does not interface with VONAPP, it does pull in the appropriate information from VADIR. The VCE verifies and changes any data in LTS, as required, based on the eligibility verification research. Once LTS has been populated, the VCE adjudicates the claim in BDN.

VA has established additional processes to ensure accurate claims processing. After the VCE completes processing of the COE in LTS but before the COE is mailed to the individual, a second VCE or Senior VCE must authorize the original claim. The authorizer reviews the records in TIMS and LTS to ensure the verification and research was done fully and accurately in accordance with policy and law. In addition to the authorization step, each RPO has a procedure for checking a certain number of claims per VCE per month to ensure accuracy.

Once the original claim has been authorized, the VCE may print and mail the COE letter. The COE states that the individual is entitled to benefits for an approved program of education or training under the Post-9/11 GI Bill; instructs the individual to take the COE to the school; informs the individual that the school must certify the individual's enrollment in order to receive payments; confirms the individual's qualifying and non-qualifying periods of active duty service; and indicates the individual's benefit level, remaining entitlement, delimiting date, and Kicker entitlement. If the individual's proposed program of education is not approved for GI Bill purposes, the VCE may customize the COE to indicate this. Finally, the COE describes the individual's right to appeal the decision and describes the process steps required for an appeal.

Processing Speed/Time

In FY2014, the VA processed original claims in an average of 17 days.[38] The processing time has decreased from 39 days in 2010 as the VA has implemented improved technology systems, primarily the LTS, and proactive caseload and process monitoring and improvements.[39]

Pell Grants

Data submitted on a FAFSA or through FAA Access is processed by the ED Central Processing System (CPS). CPS is an automated system that processes all applications for HEA Title IV aid (see box below). It performs several processes fundamental to Pell Grant processing: verifying eligibility, calculating the Expected Family Contribution (EFC), and notifying applicants and institutions of applicant eligibility. CPS is operated, maintained, and managed by an ED contractor.

Central Processing System (CPS) Components

CPS comprises a number of technological and operational components:

- The Business Intelligence (BI) Tool is an analytical tool used for the Management Information System (MIS)/Business Objectives (BO) reporting. It provides a system for reporting on HEA Title IV system activity to ED Office of Federal Student Aid (FSA) senior staff. The reports provide decision-making tools for monitoring and evaluating all HEA Title IV programs.
- FAFSA On The Web (FOTW) provides financial aid offices, students, and other authorized agents with online access to the FAFSA. It provides the following major functionalities: electronic submissions of FAFSA applications, Renewal Applications (ROTW), FAFSA Corrections on the Web (COTW), and use of FAA Access to CPS Online.
- FAFSA4caster provides students with early financial planning by estimating the federal financial aid eligibility and a sample award

package. FAFSA4caster calculates an estimated family contribution (EFC) and the sample award package using the EFC formula and loan/grant limits based on current and projected information.

- The Eligibility Determination System (EDS) processes HEA Title IV aid applicant data and provides communications between students, postsecondary schools, and the FSA office. The EDS must interact with various federal and state agencies, postsecondary institutions, private agencies serving the financial aid community, students and their families, and federal contractors. The EDS calculates the EFC.
- The Institutional Student Information Record (ISIR) Analysis (IA) Tool is designed to help schools conduct an in-depth analysis of applicant populations so they can understand the effectiveness of their own eligibility verification procedures.
- FAA Access to CPS Online consists of Student Inquiry, ISIR Requests Return of Title IV Funds (R2T4), ISIR Analysis (IA) Tool, and Application/Correction Entry. These functions assist Financial Aid Administrators (FAAs) with administering the HEA Title IV aid programs.
- The Image and Data Capture (IDC) component scans paper financial aid documents (FAFSAs, Student Aid Reports (SARs), and miscellaneous correspondence) and data entry, and electronically transmits the data and related images to the CPS mainframe for processing.
- PIN Application components provide system authentication for access. Student applicants and their parents can view financial data or sign web applications electronically.
- Student Authentication Network (STAN) provides web-based authentication using the PIN.
- The CPS Printing component prints and mails all CPS related letters and correspondence such as PIN, PIN registration reject and reauthorization letters, SARs, SAR Acknowledges, subsequent application, renewal reminder, and FAFSA4caster Social Security Administration (SSA) match rejection letters to applicants.
- Participation Management (PM) consists of the PM Web and PM Mainframe. The PM Web allows users to enroll for electronic access to FSA data. Users gain access to CPS and ED's National

Student Loan Data System (NSLDS). The PM Mainframe processes the daily transmission of PIN requests, FAFSA transaction data, and authentication to FAA Access to CPS Online.

- EDExpress Suite is PC-based software that provides for the Electronic Data Exchange (EDE) of FAFSA data between schools, state agencies, and the FSA.
- IRS Datashare allows users to access from their filed federal tax return the following information: tax payer names (first and last), tax year, Social Security number, filing status, adjusted gross income (AGI), taxes paid, type of tax return filed (1040, 1040A, etc.), number of exemptions claimed, education credits, IRS deductions, tax exempt interest income, untaxed portion of pensions, and untaxed IRS distributions. Users may print, save, copy and paste, or transfer the data directly into the online FAFSA.

Source: Calvin Whitaker, *Privacy Impact Assessment For Central Processing System (CPS)*, U.S. Department of Education, March 25, 2013; and U.S. Department of Education, Federal Student Aid, *User Guide: ISIR Analysis Tool*, January 10, 2011, http://ifap.ed.gov/qahome/iatooltraining.html.

Eligibility Verification

CPS matches and edits the data from the FAFSA in order to determine the student's eligibility for HEA Title IV aid programs, including Pell Grants. The data are checked for inconsistencies and matched against existing personal data held by ED, the Social Security Administration (SSA), the VA, DOD, Department of Justice (DOJ), Department of Homeland Security (DHS), and Selective Service System. ED maintains computer matching agreements with each federal agency in order to complete the verification. Some mistakes and inconsistencies will be overwritten by CPS.

ED Calculated EFC

The financial information on the FAFSA is used by CPS to calculate the EFC of the applicant's family. The EFC is the amount that, according to the federal need analysis methodology, can be expected to be contributed by a student's family toward the student's cost of education over a nine-month period during the upcoming award year.[40] The calculation is prescribed in statutory provisions. The student's family may consist of (1) the student alone; (2) the student and spouse; (3) the student, spouse, and dependents; (4) the student and dependents; or (5) the parents/stepparents and parents' dependents, including the student. The calculation is based on consideration of available income and, for some families, available assets as reported on the FAFSA.

There are three basic EFC formulas that may be applied depending on the type of applicant:

- those who are considered dependent on their parents;
- independent students with no dependents, other than a spouse (if any); and
- independent students with dependents other than a spouse (e.g., children).

Generally, EFC is calculated on the basis of income and assets, using various assumptions defined in statutory provisions, and adjusted for the number of family members in college. The asset contribution is not included if the family income is less than $50,000[41] and one of the following apply: a family member received means-tested federal benefits;[42] the family was eligible to file or filed certain federal income tax returns; or a student, spouse, or parent is a dislocated worker.[43]

Three groups of individuals may receive an automatic zero EFC. Otherwise Pell Grant-eligible dependent students and independent students with dependents other than a spouse can qualify for an automatic zero EFC if 2013 family income[44] was $24,000 or less[45] and one of the following apply: a family member received means-tested federal benefits; the family was eligible to file or filed certain federal income tax returns; or a student, spouse, or parent was a dislocated worker. Individuals who had a parent or guardian die as a result of military service in the U.S. Armed Forces in Iraq or Afghanistan after September 11, 2001, and who were under 24 years old or were enrolled at an IHE at the time of the parent's or guardian's death qualify for

- an automatic zero EFC if Pell Grant-eligible; or
- an Iraq and Afghanistan Service Grant (IASG), if they would otherwise be Pell Grant-eligible but for their EFC.[46]

Student Aid Report (SAR) and Institutional Student Information Record (ISIR)

Once the FAFSA is checked, CPS produces two output documents (posting, or printing and mailing, as required). CPS provides each applicant with a Student Aid Report (SAR) by mail or by email with instructions on how to access the report online. CPS also provides each IHE designated by the applicant on the FAFSA with an Institutional Student Information Record (ISIR) accessible to the FAA through FAA Access to CPS Online.

The SAR and ISIR contain the application data, results of the data matches and any inconsistencies, and the EFC if calculable. Depending on the EFC, the SAR will indicate whether the student may be eligible to receive a federal Pell Grant and other federal student aid. If a sufficient problem is found with the matches and checks, the SAR and ISIR will indicate that the student's record needs to be amended in order to receive aid. The SAR also informs the student of the next steps, including the need for updated tax information and the school completing the financial aid process. In addition, the SAR shows graduation, retention, and transfer rates for the schools selected and the total amount of federal student loans owed by the applicant.[47]

Processing Speed/Time

FAFSAs submitted electronically are processed within 3-5 days, and paper FAFSAs are processed within 7-10 days. The SAR is often available within 3-5 days online but may take as long as three weeks after submitting the FAFSA if provided by mail, depending on the method of FAFSA submission and whether an email address was submitted.

SECONDARY PROCESSING (SUPPLEMENTAL CLAIMS)/DISBURSEMENT OF FUNDS

Once initial claim and application processing determine eligibility, intervention by the prospective or actual educational institution or training establishment is integral in secondary processing, which may lead to a disbursement or payment of benefit funds.

Post-9/11 GI Bill

As soon as an individual's eligibility for Post-9/11 GI Bill benefits has been certified and the individual either enrolls in or completes a portion of education or training, VA may process payments (supplemental claims) on behalf of the eligible individual according to the processes outlined below. The educational institution or individual must certify enrollment. The payments are a mix of up-front lump sum payments and payments that support completed portions of education or training.

Certification of Enrollment by the Educational Institution

The educational institution must certify the individual's enrollment to the VA. This section describes the school certifications required for individuals pursuing non-college degree[48] and degree programs not by correspondence. The School Certifying Official (SCO) at the educational institution is notified by the individual of the desire to use GI Bill benefits either in person or through some institution-developed form or process. The SCO may be in the student services center, the financial aid office, the veterans' services center, or another office of the educational institution. If available, the individual provides a copy of the COE to the SCO, thus expediting the process. If an individual does not have a COE, the process of determining eligibility as initiated by the individual and the processing of payments as initiated by the educational institution may occur concurrently.

The SCO certifies the student's enrollment by completing a certificate of enrollment (Cert) in the VA-Online Certification of Enrollment (VA-ONCE). VA-ONCE is a VA Internet-based application used to certify student enrollment and submit Notices of Change in Student Status for VA education benefits. The Cert requires

- the individual's identifying information;
- the type of training (undergraduate degree, non-college degree, or graduate degree);
- the name of the approved program of education;
- the individual's educational objective (e.g., associate of art degree, associate of science degree, master of art degree, or non-degree);
- the number of resident training[49] credits in which the student is enrolled, the number of distance learning credits in which the student is enrolled, the number of clock hours per week, and the number of residential remedial or deficiency credits;
- the number of credits considered to be full-time by the institution, if graduate training is being pursued;
- dates of the academic term or program (if not on a term basis) including breaks; and

- the applicable net in-state tuition and fee charges, and if applicable out-of-state tuition and fee charges[50] and available Yellow Ribbon payment.[51]

The applicable net in-state tuition and fee charges are such charges reduced for DOD tuition assistance (TA) benefits,[52] and reduced for any waivers, scholarships, or other assistance that is designated for the sole purpose of reducing a student's tuition and fee cost and provided directly to the institution, except Pell Grants and loans.[53] The applicable fees are mandatory charges and thus exclude optional fees for such activities as study abroad, parking, or penalties.

The SCO may only certify applicable courses. Only courses and subjects that apply to the student's program of education may be certified,[54] and audited courses cannot be certified. Institutionally required remedial and deficiency courses may be certified.[55] The SCO may certify courses that an individual repeats in order to meet the institution's completion criteria. An individual may request that the SCO certify fewer credits than actually enrolled in in order to preserve entitlement.

SCOs may be required to include various notes in the remarks section of VA-ONCE in special circumstances. There are standard remark terms and free space for other circumstances. Remarks are required for students enrolled in cooperative programs, incarcerated as a result of a felony conviction, or enrolled in practical training or student teaching.

An individual may enroll in more than one institution in pursuit of an educational objective. The primary or parent institution must verify that the individual will take specified courses at the other named institution(s) for credit at the primary institution. The secondary institution(s) may subsequently certify the individual's actual enrollment in VA-ONCE and indicate the individual's primary institution. The secondary institution(s) may only certify the courses by the primary institution.

In order to expedite processing and ensure timely benefit payments, the VA encourages educational institutions to submit Certs for each academic term as early as possible even if the institution cannot submit tuition and fee charges until later. The SCO may certify multiple terms at one time, especially when the terms may overlap.[56] In the event that the Post-9/11 GI Bill participant does not inform the educational institution in a timely manner that he or she would like to use GI Bill benefits, the SCO may certify up to one year after the education or training.

Additional Certifications

Also as part of the initial enrollment certification, educational institutions, training establishments, and individuals must certify vocational flight training, apprenticeships or on-the-job training, tutorial assistance, correspondence training, licensing and certification tests, national tests, and relocation. These certifications and related agreements are supported through VA-ONCE, paper forms, and other communications. The administrative processes for these forms of education and training are detailed in **Appendix C** because the processes represent a small portion of Post-9/11 GI Bill participants and funding and these forms of education and training (with the exception of correspondence) are not comparable to those permitted for Pell Grant awards. Please note, however, that these forms of education and training affect the processes and systems developed and implemented by the VA to administer the Post-9/11 GI Bill program.

Educational Institution and Training Establishment Recordkeeping

The educational institutions and training establishments are required to maintain a file on each individual and his/her educational or training progress. The file must contain the documents required by statutory provisions, regulations, and other instructions. These documents include, but are not limited to, a record of all VA paperwork, school transcripts, academic records, grade reports, drop slips, registration slips (for those courses dropped during drop/add), tuition and fee charges, transcripts from previous schools with evaluations of same, the student's school application, records of disciplinary action, a program outline, a curriculum guide or graduation evaluation form, graduation or program completion, and any other pertinent forms and information.

Processing of Certifications

Once the educational institution, training establishment, or individual certifies the individual's enrollment, training, or expenditure, the RPO verifies eligibility and processes the payment, if eligible. Some Certs are processed automatically by LTS; the remainder require VCE intervention. Generally, individual VCEs only process certain kinds of Certs, reflecting the diversity of processes. For example, a VCE may specialize in test fee certifications.

The information from Certs entered in VA-ONCE is automatically populated into LTS and TIMS. Certs that request tuition and fees, Yellow Ribbon payments, housing allowances, reenlistment incentives, and books and supplies and that do not include remarks may be automatically processed, including payment calculations and payment notification letter printing. Mailing the letters is still a manual process. The automated calculations may include awards for overlapping terms. The payment amounts are transferred from LTS to BDN to make the actual payments.

If there are remarks in the VA-ONCE Cert or issues arise in the automated processing, a VCE will complete processing. The VCE may re-verify the claimant's eligibility as if issuing a COE to update any changes, resolve any discrepancies, and properly populate LTS and BDN.

The educational objective, prior education and training, and professional licenses may be used by the VCE to ensure the objective is not prohibited by statutory provisions, ensure the individual has not already achieved the objective, ensure the program of education leads to the objective, limit changes in the program of education, and ensure that the enrolled courses and pursued training are generally acceptable to meet the requirements for the objective. In addition, the VCE verifies that the program of education is approved in the Web Enabled Approval Management System (WEAMS). The program approval in WEAMS is captured in TIMS.

An award letter or denial letter is mailed to the GI Bill participant for every Cert processed. The letters may be generated by LTS or constructed with a template from PCGL and information from BDN and LTS. The award letter provides recent payments, remaining benefits, and contact information. It describes the individual's qualifying active duty service and resulting benefit level. It also summarizes the enrollment and program of education charges submitted on Certs during the academic year, describes how payment amounts were determined, and presents the amounts and timing of each payment type issued. Finally, the letter provides contact information in the event that the individual has questions and describes the individual's right to appeal, including the process.

When processing Certs, VCEs may also need to incorporate information received by email on the outcome of compliance surveys (audits). Audits, conducted by the VA and SAAs, are designed to ensure that educational institutions, training establishments, and approved courses are in compliance with all applicable provisions of the law governing GI Bills. The audit may result in restrictions on Cert processing.

Payments

Post-9/11 GI Bill payments are processed, determined, and calculated by LTS once authorized by LTS or a VCE. LTS is programmed with rules based on statutory provisions and regulations to calculate the variety of payments authorized. Authorized payments may be available for tuition and fees, the Yellow Ribbon program, a housing allowance, a books and supplies stipend, tutorial assistance, test fees, relocation and travel assistance, and Kickers. Kickers are additional benefit amounts that supplement the housing allowance of eligible Post-9/11 GI Bill participants. Payment eligibility and amounts depend on the individual's benefit level, the program of education (e.g., program leading to a degree, vocational flight, test fee, etc.), rate of pursuit,[57] institutional control and location, type of institution (institution of higher learning,[58] vocational flight school, etc.), other tuition and fees benefits, educational delivery mechanism (distance or in-residence), duty status (active duty or otherwise) of the qualifying individual, number of days in education/training for the month, need for tutorial assistance, test fee, Kicker contract, Yellow Ribbon agreement, residence and the residence's relationship to the educational institution, and the relationship to the qualifying individual. See Table 3 for the maximum amounts for tuition and fees, housing, and books and supplies for the academic year beginning August 1, 2014.

Table 3. Maximum Payment Amounts for Post-9/11 GI Bill: 2014 Academic Year (August 1, 2014-July 31, 2015)

Type of Payment	Maximum Amount[a]	Frequency
Tuition and Fees	At a public educational institution, in-state tuition and fees	Per academic term
	At a private or foreign educational institution, $20,235.02	Per academic year
Yellow Ribbon Payment	Half of the difference between net tuition and fees charged and the tuition and fees benefit[b]	Per academic term or year
Housing Allowance	E-5 with dependents BAHc in the military housing area in which the educational institution is located	Per month
Books and Supplies Stipend	$1,000	Per academic year

Type of Payment	Maximum Amount[a]	Frequency
Tutorial Assistance	$1,200	Per entitlement period
Fees for National Tests and Licensing and Certification Tests	$2,000	Per test
Relocation and Travel Assistance	$500	One time
Supplemental Assistance/Kickers	$950	Per month

Source: Compiled by CRS based on U.S. Code and Department of Veterans Affairs, Education and Training, Rate Tables available at http://www.benefits.va.gov/GIBILL/resources/benefits_resources/rate_tables.asp.

[a] The maximum amount is subject to reduction according to statutory provisions. Payments for many individuals will be lower than the maximum payments shown above based on the individual's length of qualifying active duty service, enrollment rate or rate of pursuit, active duty status, actual charges, being enrolled exclusively through distance learning, and receipt of DOD Tuition Assistance (TA). Under TA, military service branches may pay a certain amount of tuition and expenses for the education and training of active duty personnel and members of the Selected Reserve.

[b] The VA and the institution of higher learning (IHL) each pay half of the difference between some portion of the tuition and fees charged and the tuition and fees benefit depending on the Yellow Ribbon agreement between the VA and IHL.

[c] The E-5 with dependents BAH is the monthly basic allowance for housing for a member of the Armed Forces with dependents in pay grade E-5.

Payment timing also differs. Generally, payments are made at the beginning of the month for the previous month. Payments may be delayed to subsequent months if there is a delay in processing or certification. The Payment History Inquiry Screen (TINQ) in the "SHARE" system, an automated computer system that maintains claim receipt dates and benefit payment dates, indicates when payments are made. The VA's call center may review SHARE to determine recent benefit information.

Tuition and Fees and Yellow Ribbon (YR) Payments to Institutions

In most instances, the tuition and fees and YR payments are sent to the institution by check or Electronic Funds Transfer (EFT).[59] The tuition and fees and YR payments may be sent up to two weeks before the start of the academic term or once the Cert has been processed. In most instances, the individual's Post-9/11 GI Bill entitlement is charged one day for each day the individual is enrolled full-time (or the equivalent for part-time enrollment). The VA also mails each institution a weekly Vet Rep Listing Report, which lists all the individuals and payments (tuition and fees and YR payments) made directly to the institution.

Payments to Eligible Individuals

Other than payments covering tuition and fees charges, payments are made directly to the eligible individuals by check or EFT. Post-9/11 GI Bill-eligible individuals may receive one or more of the following payments directly:

- a monthly housing allowance at the beginning of each month for the previous month(s);
- the books and supplies stipend at the beginning of each academic term;
- tutorial assistance in a lump sum upon completion of tutoring;
- supplemental assistance and Kickers added to the housing allowance at the beginning of each month for the previous month(s);[60]
- test fees in a lump sum after test administration;
- relocation and travel assistance in a one-time lump sum upon certification; and
- a refund of contributions to the MGIB-AD in a one-time lump sum added to the final housing allowance paid when the individual's entitlement is exhausted.

Processing Speed/Time

As of December 2014, the LTS processed over 50% of supplemental claims received electronically from end-to-end within one day of receipt.[61] In FY2014, the VA processed supplemental claims for returning students in an average of six days.[62]

On average, educational institutions submitted certifications for 60 Post-9/11 GI Bill recipients in academic year 2010-2011; although 13% of educational institutions certified fewer than three Post-9/11 GI Bill recipients in academic year 2010-2011.[63]

Pell Grant and Title IV Aid Packaging

After initial processing of FAFSA is complete, Pell Grants are administered by IHEs concurrently with other HEA Title IV aid and often with state, institutional, and other aid. Every institution that administers HEA Title IV aid must maintain policies and procedures that govern its process for verification that are consistent with the federal statutory and regulatory provisions. IHEs are responsible for reporting suspected cases of intentional misrepresentation or fraud to ED's Office of Inspector General.

The students' point of contact at the IHE is the financial aid administrator (FAA). The FAA may receive the SAR or ISIR in FAA Access to CPS Online for an applicant, registering student, or currently enrolled student and begin secondary processing.

Secondary Eligibility Verification

There are three scenarios that require a student's eligibility to be reviewed. If the SAR or ISIR indicate critical inconsistencies, the applicant or FAA must correct the inconsistencies on the FAFSA, or the applicant must provide to the FAA original and adequate documentation such that the FAA can override the CPS error codes. The IHE is ultimately responsible for resolving discrepancies prior to the disbursement of any federal aid and ensuring proper Pell Grant payments. In addition to the initial CPS eligibility verification, CPS and each IHE select a number of applications for additional verification.[64] If an application is chosen for verification, the applicant must present supporting documentation to the FAA.

Pell Grant Award

An eligible student's annual Pell Grant award is determined on the basis of a set of award rules defined in statute and regulations that use the student's EFC, cost of attendance (COA), enrollment status, maximum Pell Grant award, and minimum Pell Grant award.

COA is a measure of a student's educational expenses for the period of enrollment. For Pell Grant purposes, the period of enrollment is always based on full-time attendance for a full academic year (e.g., 12 credit hours per semester for two semesters requiring at least 30 weeks of total instruction). Statutory provisions determine the types of costs included in COA,[65] and the IHE and FAA determine the appropriate and reasonable amounts of those costs. Examples of the permissible types of expenses, depending on the student's circumstances, are tuition and fees; books, supplies, transportation, and miscellaneous personal expenses; room and board;[66] and dependent care.

The maximum Pell Grant award for each award year is specified in the annual appropriations act and HEA.[67] For award year 2014-2015, the total maximum Pell Grant is $5,730. For award year 2014-2015, the minimum Pell Grant award, as defined in HEA, is 10% of the total maximum Pell Grant award.[68]

In some instances, the FAA may use professional judgment to adjust COA and/or data used to calculate EFC. The FAA may use discretion and adequate documentation to adjust for a student's individual and special circumstances. For example, an adjustment may be made to accommodate unusual healthcare costs or recent unemployment. Professional judgment may not be used to change the letter or intent of the statutory provisions or regulations governing aid administration.

To calculate the Pell Grant award amount for the full award year, the FAA can enter the COA, EFC, and expected enrollment status in a software program, such as EDExpress, to calculate the award or manually access payment schedules published by ED. EDExpress is available free of charge from ED to IHEs to process and manage federal student aid records (see box).

EDExpress

EDExpress is a financial aid management software package that allows FAAs to manage HEA Title IV aid application data, package awards, and exchange data with the Common Origination and Disbursement (COD) System for Direct Loans, Pell Grants, and the Teacher Education Assistance for College and Higher Education (TEACH) Grant Program. ED provides EDExpress and the communications software, EDconnect, free of charge to Electronic Data Exchange (EDE) participants.

The EDExpress software is available with the following modules:

- Global: The Global module provides core features and functionality for EDExpress as a whole. It also enables FAAs to create and print user-defined data.
- App Express: The App Express module allows FAAs to create, correct, review, print, export, and import student financial aid records. The module interfaces with FAA Access to CPS Online.
- Packaging: The Packaging module enables FAAs to track, package, award, and manage financial aid awards. The module can

be customized to apply each IHE's award methodologies.

- Direct Loan: The Direct Loan module lets FAAs create loan origination records, print promissory notes, and post actual disbursements for processing by the Common Origination and Disbursement (COD). COD is an ED system that allows IHEs to request, report, and reconcile HEA Title IV funds with ED.
- Pell Grant: The Pell module lets FAAs create Pell Grant origination and disbursement records and process Pell Grant data through COD.
- TEACH: The TEACH module allows FAAs to create, export, and import TEACH Grant origination and disbursement records and process data through COD.

EDExpress also contains global functionality (such as Security setup and Compact and Repair Database) that is not related exclusively to one of the modules mentioned above.

Source: U.S. Department of Education, Federal Student Aid, *2015-2016 Desk Reference for EDExpress for Windows Release 1.0*; U.S. Department of Education, Federal Student Aid, *Technical Reference for Electronic Data Exchange (EDE) 2014-2015*; and U.S. Department of Education, Federal Student Aid, *Installation Guide for EDExpress for Windows 2015- 2016.*

Once the FAA determines the student's Pell Grant award for the full award year, the FAA calculates the amount(s) to disburse during the award year based on the student's attendance pattern. Pell Grants must be paid in installments over the award year. A student receives a Pell Grant only for the payment period (e.g., academic term) for which he/she is enrolled. For example, a student who enrolls full time for two semesters during a standard trimester award year will receive at least two Pell Grant disbursements, one for each semester, totaling the student's Pell Grant award for the full award year. Conversely, a student who enrolls full time for only one semester during a standard trimester award year receives one disbursement equal to approximately one-half of the Pell Grant award for the full award year. And finally, a student who enrolls full-time for three semesters (fall, spring, and summer) during a standard trimester award year will receive at least two Pell Grant payments, typically one each for the fall and spring semesters.

Title IV Aid Package

After calculating the Pell Grant award, the FAA will *package* the remainder of the student's Title IV aid. Packaging is a process by which the FAA combines HEA Title IV aid, institutional aid, employer education assistance, private loans, and other aid from non-federal sources such as states to meet the financial need of students and cover the students' educational costs. The federal components of the package are determined by HEA Title IV statute and regulations and IHE policies and philosophy. The Pell Grant or IASG award is considered the first source (foundation) of the package. Software, such as EDExpress and those programs offered by commercial vendors, may facilitate packaging. A full description of aid packaging is outside the scope of this report.

The full package of various aid sources and amounts is presented to each student in an award letter. Educational funds that are not part of the aid package include GI Bill benefits,[69] vocational rehabilitation assistance, Senior Reserve Officers' Training Corps (ROTC) scholarships (Title 10 U.S.C., Chapter 103), and some additional non-Title IV aid. The student and parents, if applicable, with the assistance of the FAA, if requested, must choose which aid within the package to accept. The IHE must disseminate information to ensure student aid applicants are notified of the terms and conditions of aid programs, sources and amounts of aid offered, the method for disbursing and applying aid, student's rights and responsibilities, institutional processes, and other Title IV-required disclosures of consumer information.[70]

Processing Payments

If a student accepts a Pell Grant or IASG, the FAA disburses the funds according to schedule and records the disbursements in the Common Origination and Disbursement (COD) system. COD is an ED system to which IHEs have access in order to request, report, and reconcile HEA Title IV funds. Pell Grant awards and disbursements must be recorded in COD. Before the actual disbursement, the FAA must confirm that the student remains eligible, has received any required information disclosures, and is enrolled in or attending the IHE, as required.

The IHE has some flexibility in the schedule for disbursing Pell Grant funds.[71] Assuming the student applies and is determined eligible in a timely manner, the disbursements may occur up to 10 days prior to the start of the payment period but not before the student completes the prior payment period. For example, an IHE may choose to disburse funds after the course add/drop date. The IHE also has the flexibility to provide each disbursement to a student in multiple installments if it is in the best interest of the student.

The disbursement may be deposited in the student's school account or paid directly to the student or family. Most IHEs deposit the funds in the student's account. After crediting a student's account with Pell Grant funds, the IHE will deduct from the account unpaid tuition, fees, and institutionally provided room and board due for the current program year. Any remaining Pell Grant funds may be paid directly to the student for personal use. In general, the remaining funds must be paid or made available to the student or family within 14 days.

School Administration of Pell Grant Funds

In addition to ensuring student eligibility and calculating Pell Grant awards, IHEs are responsible for proper management of Pell Grant funds and associated recordkeeping and disclosures. ED has developed two basic methods for disbursing Pell Grant funds to IHEs: ED may obligate the funds to the IHE upfront or reimburse the IHE for disbursements.[72]

In the upfront approach used by most IHEs, ED establishes an authorization of Pell Grant funding in COD against which an IHE may request (draw down) funds. The authorization level is based on actual disbursement records accepted by the COD system. Once the IHE draws down funds, it must make payments to students as soon as administratively feasible but no later than three business days after receiving (drawing down) the funds from ED.[73]

IHEs for which ED has a concern about their ability to meet Title IV participation requirements may receive funds from ED through *Reimbursement* or one of the *Cash Monitoring* payment methods. Under these methods the IHE is paid back for funds it has disbursed to students.

IHEs receive Pell Grant funds and other Title IV funds by electronic funds transfer (EFT) using ED's G5 payment system. G5 is an electronic grants management and payments system that supports the planning, obligating, authorizing, disbursing, and final closing of ED grant awards and payments. After the school awards all the Pell Grant funds due to students, the school returns any remainder to ED.

The IHE must have policies and procedures in place to ensure proper management of HEA Title IV funds. Information must be shared between offices and departments within the IHE. Each IHE must designate a coordinating official to ensure Title IV aid is administered correctly; however, no single person or office may authorize payment and disburse or deliver Title IV funds.

As described, IHEs must make several notifications to students and parents throughout the financial aid process. Most notifications and disclosures may be sent and authorizations received electronically by schools unless regulations specifically require the use of U.S. mail. Voluntary consent to participate in electronic transactions is required for all notices and authorizations to HEA Title IV aid recipients.

Processing Speed/Time

Processing speed is determined by the availability of FAAs and IHE internal systems for processing. On average, there were 1,653 Pell Grant recipients for each IHE that awarded Pell Grants in award year 2011-2012.[74]

SUBSEQUENT OR ADJUSTED PAYMENTS

After payment(s) for the initial academic term or pursuit have been distributed, subsequent payments may be distributed or previous payments adjusted. Both the Post-9/11 GI Bill program and Pell Grant program have processes to ensure subsequent payments are made properly and adjustments are made to match the student's circumstances and the programs' objectives.

Post-9/11 GI Bill

Educational institutions, training establishments, and individuals must certify enrollment or pursuit every academic term, month, year, or program, depending on the type of education and training. Once the supplemental claim is approved for an academic term at an educational institution for a program other than by correspondence, LTS automatically approves and initiates subsequent payments for the housing allowance and books and supplies stipend throughout the certification period unless there is a change to the certification. Payments for completed education and training (i.e., tutorial assistance) are processed by the RPO as described above upon receipt of a Cert.

In most instances, an individual need not reapply to continue receiving benefits.[75] In addition to the regular certification of enrollment, an educational institution may need to correct or revise a previous Cert if the participant's rate of pursuit changes, the participant fails to maintain satisfactory academic progress or conduct, the participant takes a leave of absence or terminates enrollment, or the participant receives an incomplete grade. The changes should be reported within 30 days or as soon as possible. Depending on the change, the SCO may *adjust* the number of hours, *amend* the term dates or charges, or *terminate* an individual's attendance. The SCO must maintain a change record in the student's file.

Based on the adjustment, amendment, or termination; reason; and effective date, VA recalculates the benefits for which the participant is eligible for the academic term. If the benefit amounts increase, the next payment(s) will reflect the increased amount that was not received previously. If the benefit amounts decrease, the next payment(s) will reflect the decreased amount but not make up for overpayments received previously.

Satisfactory Academic Progress or Conduct

The educational institution must notify the VA if a GI Bill participant is placed on academic probation or is not making satisfactory progress and is terminated or has been suspended or dismissed for unsatisfactory progress, attendance, or conduct. Notification of placement on academic probation is provided through the VA's "Ask a Question" via the Internet Inquiry System (Right Now Web). Notification of unsatisfactory progress, attendance, or conduct is made through VA-ONCE. The VA encourages educational institutions and training establishments to notify the GI Bill participants of counseling and tutorial assistance available through the institution or establishment and the VA. Likewise, the VA will reach out to the individual to offer assistance. Educational institutions and training establishments are responsible for defining and enforcing their standards of academic progress, attendance, and conduct. Participants are not eligible for benefits for periods during which they are not pursuing an approved program of education.

Individuals on academic probation may continue to receive GI Bill benefits. Individuals who are not making satisfactory progress cannot receive GI Bill benefits until the issue is resolved with the educational institution. To resume receiving benefits, the individual may re-enroll in the same program at the same institution under the terms of the institution. The reasons for resumption are recorded in the individual's student file. Alternatively, the individual may submit a Request for Change of Program or Place of Training to the VA to gain approval for a change of program, which is more suitable to the individual, once the reason for prior unsatisfactory progress is resolved.[76]

Change of Program or Place of Training

For GI Bill participants who desire to change educational institutions or training establishments or change educational objective, the change must be recorded and approved. The participant must submit a Request for Change of Program or Place of Training to VA to gain approval for a change of program. Participants changing educational institutions or training establishments submit the form manually to the SCO for retention in the student's file.

If a student changes his/her program while enrolled at the same educational institution, a record of the change must be recorded in the student's file and changed in VA-ONCE. The student does not need to notify VA through the Change of Program form.

Pell Grant

To be eligible for a Pell Grant in a subsequent academic year, a prospective student or ongoing student must complete a FAFSA each subsequent academic year for which they would like to receive HEA Title IV aid. For students who submitted a FAFSA the prior year, FAFSA on the Web can prefill prior-year information (Renewal FAFSA) to simplify the submission process. In contiguous subsequent years, students must maintain satisfactory academic progress (see description below) and may renew their FAFSA online by correcting any items that have changed. Most students receive a system-generated renewal reminder by email or regular mail in January or February if they received aid in that same academic year. After the student submits FAFSA for a subsequent academic year, CPS verifies eligibility and calculates the student's EFC, and the FAA calculates COA, packages the student's aid, and disburses payments.

To receive additional Pell Grant funds during a single academic year, the FAA may need to release additional installments during the academic term, release additional disbursements for subsequent payment periods (payment periods are usually the academic term) in the same academic year, and adjust or re-estimate the aid package. To be eligible for a second Pell Grant disbursement during a single academic year, a student generally must maintain satisfactory academic progress (see description below). Disbursements for subsequent payment periods in the same academic year may occur after 10 days prior to the start of the payment period but not before the student completes the prior payment period. For clock-hour programs and nonterm credit-hour programs, disbursement for the second payment period occurs when the student successfully completes 50% of the weeks of instructional time and 50% of the credit-hours/clockhours in the academic year or program or the remaining portion of a program that is more than one-half of an academic year but less than a full academic year. Any adjustments and disbursements must be recorded in COD.

There are few instances in which IHEs are required to recalculate the Pell award for the current or subsequent payment periods. If the EFC is corrected mid-payment period or if the student fails to attend at least one day in one or more classes, the Pell award for the current payment period must be recalculated. The recalculation may lead to an additional disbursement for the payment period, an adjustment to the disbursement for a subsequent payment period in the same award year, or an overpayment. If a student's enrollment rate changes from one payment period to the next payment period in the same award year, the Pell Grant disbursement for the next payment period is based on the enrollment rate in that next payment period. IHEs may establish policies to recalculate Pell Grants in other circumstances.

The FAA may need to adjust or recalculate the rest of the aid package in the event that the student's circumstances change. Common changes include

- a finding that the student is ineligible,
- the student receiving more aid than allowed by the program,
- the aid exceeding the student's financial need,
- the aid exceeding the student's COA,
- the enrollment status of a student changes,
- the student's EFC being adjusted in the middle of an award year, or
- the student receiving more financial assistance than originally estimated.

The adjustment or recalculation may result in an *overaward.* An overaward exists when a student's aid package exceeds the amount to which the individual is eligible according to HEA. With the exception of the aforementioned circumstances, a correctly determined Pell Grant is never adjusted in a package that is overawarded. The adjustments must come from forms of aid controlled by the school other than the Pell Grant. If the overaward cannot be resolved by receiving a payment from the student or through a subsequent disbursement in the same academic year, it becomes an overpayment.

Satisfactory Academic Progress

Satisfactory academic progress is delineated by policies developed by each participating IHE, but these policies must meet minimum federal standards. Federal standards require a minimum GPA or the equivalent and successful completion of courses at a pace to ensure successful program completion in a maximum timeframe, which is usually 150% of the program's published duration. Students enrolled in programs of more than two years must also at the end of the second year have a GPA of C or better, its equivalent, or the IHE's graduation requirement.

With two exceptions, students who fail to make satisfactory academic progress are not eligible for Pell Grants in the subsequent payment period—academic year or payment period for one-year or less-than-one-year programs. Students may regain Pell Grant eligibility by making satisfactory academic progress in a subsequent payment period. After failing to make satisfactory academic progress, a student may regain eligibility in the immediately subsequent payment period if placed on financial aid probation or warning. Students who fail to make satisfactory academic progress as a result of special circumstances and who are likely to be able to make satisfactory academic progress in the future may appeal, if the IHE permits appeals, and be placed on financial aid probation in order to be Pell Grant eligible in the immediately subsequent payment period.[77] IHEs may place students on financial aid warning for a single payment period.

OVERPAYMENTS

The resolution of overpayments is an issue for Post-9/11 GI Bill participants and educational institutions, as well as IHEs that participate in the HEA Title IV aid programs.

Post-9/11 GI Bill

A common complaint of Post-9/11 GI Bill participants and IHLs regarding benefit administration is the incurring and resolution of overpayments. An overpayment occurs when the VA reduces a student's benefit amount after providing a payment that exceeds that amount. Overpayments most often occur when Post-9/11 GI Bill participants reduce their course enrollment rate after the VA has paid tuition and fees as a lump sum based on the higher enrollment rate. Most overpayments are the responsibility of the individual to resolve.

Educational Institution Responsibility to the VA

An educational institution may be liable for overpayments based on amounts that it received directly from the VA. (Training establishments are not generally responsible for overpayments since they do not receive payments directly from the VA.) An educational institution is liable for an overpayment of amounts received directly from the VA if the GI Bill participant fails to attend any classes, the participant withdraws on or before the first day of the term, the participant dies, the educational institution receives an erroneous payment (i.e., a duplicate payment, a payment above the certified amount, or a payment for the wrong student), or the institution submits an amended enrollment certification with reduced charges or a Yellow Ribbon amount that was not the result of the individual's change in enrollment. The law also provides a school liability provision under which the school may be liable for overpayments to the claimant if the overpayment was the result of willful or negligent improper certification.

In the event of an overpayment for which the educational institution is responsible, LTS calculates the amount of the debt, populates information in BDN, and generates a letter to the SCO regarding the nature and amount of the overpayment. Within three days, BDN automatically sends the debt information to the VA's Debt Management Center (DMC). DMC processes most debts for the VA. DMC notifies debtors by mail of their debt and the available processes for repayment. Within three days, DMC will send a Notice of Indebtedness (NOI) to the SCO explaining that the institution must resolve (repay or dispute) the debt within 30 days. Once DMC notifies the SCO, the debt must be resolved with DMC; the SCO may dispute the overpayment by contacting DMC via phone or email. Alternatively, the SCO and institution may remit the overpayment amount to DMC.

Unless the debt is resolved or disputed, DMC will send a second NOI to the SCO explaining that the institution must resolve the debt within 30 days. If the debt is not resolved within the 30 days, DMC will send a third NOI to the SCO explaining that the institution must resolve the debt within 60 days. If the debt remains unresolved within 60 days of the third NOI, DMC refers the debt to the Treasury Offset Program (TOP) for further collection. Debts referred to TOP are no longer the jurisdiction of the VA or DMC. TOP deducts the debt and an administrative fee from other federal payments that would have gone to the institution.[78] TOP remits the collected funds to DMC in order to administratively resolve the debt.

In the event that the debt is disputed, DMC, with assistance from the RPO as necessary, reviews the debt and make a decision/determination. LTS, BDN, and TIMS are updated accordingly.

VA sends monthly "School AR Reports" listing school debts to SCOs. The report lists students' names, file numbers, debt balances, and when debts were created and includes a cover letter explaining how to return payment.

Student Responsibility to VA

In most instances, GI Bill participants are responsible for overpayments related to their benefits. LTS calculates the amount of the debt, populates information in BDN, and sends a letter to the GI Bill participant regarding the nature and amount of the overpayment. The GI Bill participant is expected to contact the RPO in writing to resolve the debt. The GI Bill participant may resolve the debt by

- repaying the debt;
- requesting, in writing, a payment agreement with the VA that assures the debt will be repaid within one year;
- requesting, in writing, a waiver from all or a portion of the debt within 30 days of debt notification if the collection would be unfair and create a financial hardship and avoid the offset of future GI Bill payments for debt collection;[79]
- requesting, in writing, a waiver from all or a portion of the debt after 30 days but within 180 days of debt notification if the collection would be unfair and create a financial hardship and have future GI Bill payments offset for debt collection; or
- submitting, in writing, a compromise offer for the debt and a Financial Status Report (form available from VA by phone).

The RPO also contacts DMC. If the GI Bill participant fails to respond to the first letter within 10 days, DMC will send a demand letter. Once DMC provides notification, the debt must be resolved with DMC. Unless action is taken by the beneficiary within 30 days of creation of a debt, the VA offsets overpayments from each monthly housing stipend until recovered.[80] In addition, if the participant does not contact DMC within 30 days, DMC will send a second demand letter explaining that the GI Bill participant must resolve the debt within 30 days. If the debt is not resolved within the 30 days, DMC will send a warning letter explaining that the individual must resolve the debt within 60 days. Within 30 days of the warning letter, DMC notifies credit agencies. Within 60 days of the warning letter, DMC refers the debt to TOP. If the debt is not resolved with TOP within 60 days, it is referred to private collection agencies.

Concurrent with the VA's overpayment collection process, the educational institution will calculate any refund that the GI Bill participant will receive from or owes to the institution. The educational institution calculates any amounts and makes payments based on its policies and procedures.

Payment Error Rate and Magnitude

In 2013, VA identified $870,000 in improper payments for the Post-9/11 GI Bill, Montgomery GI Bill-Selected Reserve, and Reserve Educational Assistance programs combined.[81]

Pell Grant

An overpayment of Pell Grant funds may consist of student debt and IHE debt. The amount of student debt and IHE debt are calculated by the FAA. IHE debt must be returned to ED. The IHE is initially responsible for trying to collect from the student the amount of the student's overpayment.

School Responsibility to ED

A school is liable for any incorrect payments made to the student due to school error (i.e., not following ED regulations). For overpayments for which the school is responsible, the school is liable for the amount and for physically returning the funds. This includes administrative, filing, and processing errors. School officials may be subject to a $10,000 fine, a prison sentence, or both if they knowingly make false or misleading statements.

If an overpayment is generated, the IHE must initiate a *Return of Title IV funds* (Return) to the federal government. An IHE may calculate the amount of funds to be returned using the Return of Title IV Funds on the Web (R2T4) in FAA Access to CPS Online. The amount of the Return does not include the amount of the overpayment for which the student is responsible. IHEs must have or make arrangements for adequate cash reserves to return Title IV funds within 45 days in the event that a student withdraws. The IHE may return the funds through the G5 payment system, a check to ED, or disbursing to another eligible student. The IHE must return funds to ED within 30 days if the student fails to begin attendance. The IHE must record returned funds in COD.

The IHE may seek to regain the returned funds from the student, but this debt to the IHE does not affect a student's eligibility for future HEA Title IV aid.

Student Responsibility to the School and ED

Students are liable for any overpayments for which the IHE is not liable.[82] For example, the student will be liable for the overpayment when making a mistake on the FAFSA, providing faulty tax returns, or other scenarios where student error caused an incorrect EFC to be calculated. Also as discussed earlier in the section entitled Subsequent or Adjusted Payments, the student may be liable for an overpayment resulting from an enrollment status change after the student begins attending. If the student is liable, the IHE is responsible for trying to collect the amount of the student's overpayment. A student is not liable for overpayments under $25 if they are not a remaining balance. The school may choose to help the student repay these funds at their discretion, such as by establishing a repayment plan for the student or repaying the overpayment on behalf of the student. Two years is the maximum time a school may allow for repayment. The student is ineligible for subsequent Title IV funds until the overpayment is resolved. If the student fails to resolve the repayment within 45 days by returning or making arrangements to return the funds to the school, the IHE refers the overpayment to ED's Debt Resolution Service. ED's Debt Resolution Service helps students resolve HEA Title IV aid debt that is in defaulted status. ED provides a centralized web portal to facilitate the process. The student may negotiate overpayment collection with the Debt Resolution Service.

Payment Error Rate and Magnitude

The rate of errors that require extra or returned funds was 3.7% in 2008, falling to 3.1% in 2010. However, the dollar amount nearly doubled between the two years, from $17 billion in 2008 to $32 billion in 2010.[83]

POST-9/11 GI BILL ISSUES AND CONCERNS

This section highlights a few salient and distinctive issues and concerns regarding the administration of benefit payments under the Post-9/11 GI Bill. This information supplements the administrative process descriptions by describing some consequences and challenges associated with various process steps. Where applicable, potential opportunities to address the issues by adopting mechanisms or practices employed in the administration of Pell Grants are explored. In addition, possible limitations that may arise from applying Pell Grant administrative processes to the Post-9/11 GI Bill processes are identified in order that they may be considered and mitigated.

Participants May Not Maximize Federal Educational Assistance

Some concerns have arisen about the extent to which individuals are maximizing the value of the assistance available through both programs. Individuals who meet the eligibility requirements for the Post-9/11 GI Bill and for Pell Grants, and other HEA Title IV aid, may receive benefits from all of the programs concurrently. In 2008, Congress excluded GI Bill benefits from being counted in determining eligibility for HEA Title IV aid in order to maximize veteran eligibility for federal educational assistance.[84] In 2012, Congress enacted legislation to support "the best use of education benefits" by veterans through the provision of specified information.[85]

At the educational institution, Post-9/11 GI Bill benefits are administered by the SCO using VA systems, guidance, and forms, and Pell Grants are administered by the FAA using ED systems, guidance, and forms. Depending on the institution, the SCO and FAA may not be the same individual and may not be in the same organizational unit of the institution.

There is no statutory requirement for program coordination or intra-program consideration. Some participants and advocacy organizations are concerned that Post-9/11 GI Bill participants may not be counseled on how to maximize program benefits and minimize future loan liability.[86] This concern can be related to acceptance of Pell Grants and is often related to HEA Title IV loans. For example, a combined SCO/FAA may counsel a student to use HEA Title IV aid while pursuing an associate's degree at a community college and subsequently combine Post-9/11 GI Bill benefits and HEA Title IV aid while pursuing a bachelor's and master's degree at more expensive four-year institutions. In another example, a combined SCO/FAA may stress to a Post-9/11 GI Bill recipient that the individual may choose to accept none of or less than the maximum HEA Title IV loan for which he/she is eligible given the amount of Post-9/11 GI Bill benefits that may be received. Alternatively, this same information could be relayed directly from either the Department of Veterans Affairs or Department of Education, or both, through other disclosures and outreach. At issue is whether or not benefit recipients have a clear sense of the most advantageous sequence or combination in which to use each form of assistance.

There are options that may help beneficiaries of GI Bill benefits and HEA Title IV aid maximize those benefits. Statutory provisions could require that the SCO, FAA, and student jointly review the student's long-term educational objectives and plan and review benefits eligibility. If the SCO and FAA were the same person, consideration of both benefits may occur spontaneously; however, some expertise in the programs and focus on each target population may be lost as the SCO/FAA is required to do more. Alternatively, the administrative processes or systems could be merged to consider both forms of assistance. In 2008, Congress excluded GI Bill benefits from consideration in the calculation of HEA Title IV aid to reduce the perceived financial harm to veterans that was occurring with the coordination of benefits and thus increase college aid and support for veterans and military families.[87] Another option that could occur outside the administration of benefits is to ensure beneficiaries receive financial counseling and understand the information specific to the coordination of benefits.

Responsibility to Select, Relinquish, or Transfer Benefits

The Post-9/11 GI Bill requires many eligible individuals to make significant and sometimes irrevocable decisions and actions in order to use their benefits as desired. A lack of understanding regarding these actions or improper timing may result in unfulfilled educational objectives and unused benefits that could have been beneficial. Three key actions are the selection of the Post-9/11 GI Bill, the irrevocable election to relinquish another GI Bill, and finally the designation of dependents to which to transfer benefits.

The application form requires eligible individuals to choose the GI Bill for which they are applying. For a small minority of individuals, the Post-9/11 GI Bill is not the most advantageous GI Bill. Most individuals who serve on active duty on or after September 11, 2001, are eligible for more than one GI Bill. It is the individual's responsibility to choose the applicable and most beneficial GI Bill from which to receive benefits during the application process. The VA does make tools available through its website and the VA call center to help inform this decision if individuals choose to avail themselves of them.[88] Some stakeholders have suggested requiring that all eligible individuals receive benefit counseling prior to using their benefit; however, this may be resource intensive and may be insulting or irksome to eligible individuals who are informed.

In addition, the application form requires individuals who are also eligible for the Montgomery GI Bill-Active Duty (MGIB-AD), Montgomery GI Bill-Selected Reserve (MGIB-SR), or Reserve Educational Assistance Program (REAP) to make a dated irrevocable election to receive Post-9/11 GI Bill benefits in lieu of one of those other GI Bills. Some participants and advocacy organizations have indicated the choices may be confusing. The VA Office of Inspector General (OIG) indicates that many veterans do not know which GI Bills they are eligible for and which to relinquish.[89] Failure to relinquish a benefit or date it correctly has delayed the receipt of benefits for some individuals. The suggestion of requiring benefit counseling prior to using their benefit would also address this issue.

Servicemembers may transfer their Post-9/11 GI Bill benefits to eligible family members while serving on active duty or in the Selected Reserve, after serving at least six years, and upon promising to serve an additional four years. Some individuals have not designated any transfer or not updated the designation with new dependents while serving. This failure has disappointed some eligible individuals who have no recourse to transfer those benefits after retirement or discharge. DOD and the service branches provide some outreach to servicemembers regarding this limitation. One option for helping active duty members would be including this information in the mandatory portions of the Transition Assistance Program, which provides pre-separation services and counseling on a number of transition-related topics to separating members of the Armed Forces.

In general, Pell Grant applicants and recipients are not required to make any decisions regarding program eligibility. With respect to selecting a GI Bill and relinquishing a GI Bill, LTS or the VCE could make a default decision unless the applicant opts for an alternative. Conversely, Congress could eliminate the likelihood of individuals being eligible for multiple GI Bills by consolidating or eliminating some GI Bills.

Perhaps, the only analogous decision required of Pell Grant eligible students is the rare decision not to accept a Pell Grant award presented in their financial aid package. A savvy and informed student may choose to bank their Pell eligibility for periods of greater personal need. There is no requirement that FAAs help students discern whether to decline a Pell award because the assumption is that Pell-eligible students are financially needy.

Lack of Real-Time Claim Information

Post-9/11 GI Bill claimants and SCOs would like easily accessible real-time information on the status of claims, eligible benefit amounts, expected payment dates, or pending issues. Although a claimant and SCO can check the status of their claim by calling the VA, the VA call center is not considered easily accessible in the age of online information. eBenefits provides information on entitlement and school enrollment, but does not yet provide real-time access to information such as claim status, payment amounts, and remaining entitlement.

The HEA Title IV aid process does make more real-time information available. The status of an applicant's FAFSA (complete or incomplete data entry, selection for verification, EFC, and loans outstanding) is available online either immediately if submitted online or within 7-10 days of processing if submitted by mail. However, Pell Grant applicants are similarly limited to real-time information on the secondary school processing by calling or contacting their FAA.

Cumbersome Initial Claim Processing Systems and Accompanying Delays

Despite improved claim processing speeds since 2009, a major complaint continues to be the length of time required to process original claims, in particular. The VA has indicated that additional funds for information technology improvements could facilitate streamlining the initial claims processing. For example, VADIR lacks some service information, thus preventing an automated eligibility determination.[90] Service records for individuals in the reserves or National Guard often required additional research; however, system interfaces have been improved to reduce this.[91]

Also, for example, VONAPP and LTS are not currently interfaced.[92] In addition to system issues, claimants make errors or miss questions on the application that require the claimant's and VCE's time to resolve with proper documentation. For example, individuals may not (1) make the requisite irrevocable election, (2) date the irrevocable election properly, or (3) choose a program for which they are eligible.[93] In addition to VA processing systems, the VA Office of Inspector General (OIG) has indicated that processing delayed by the submission of inaccurate and incomplete applications (especially the selection of an irrevocable election) might be improved by better educating veterans on the form.[94]

Another issue that has arisen in all phases of Post-9/11 GI Bill claims processing is RPO and LTS errors. One example is VCEs not computing an individual's qualifying length of service properly. Another example is incorrect payment calculations as programmed into LTS.[95] A similar common audit finding by ED for HEA Title IV aid is the incorrect calculation of Pell Grant amounts by FAAs. ED suggests that IHEs improve their internal controls, training, procedures, and internal audits.[96]

The options for expediting processing and improving calculation accuracy could include information technology systems improvements, a simplification of the eligibility requirements and process steps, and improved training and resources for VCEs. For example, the HEA Title IV aid information technology systems are continually updated by ED contractors to reduce the incidence of issues and remain current with legislative changes. However, despite the mature HEA Title IV aid information technology systems, FAFSA data entry errors must be corrected manually and almost half of eligible applicants are flagged for verification of at least one application question.[97]

Administrative Burden on SCOs

The tracking and manual work required of SCOs to properly certify, including amendments, adjustments, and terminations; record payments; verify proper payments; and research issues results in an administrative burden on educational institutions and training establishments, slows the disbursement of Post-9/11 GI Bill benefits, and results in improper payments. SCOs must complete calculations for certifications and amendments, adjustments, and terminations before manually entering the requested data in VA-ONCE. Educational institutions have invested in or developed their own Post-9/11 GI

Bill application forms, software systems, or spreadsheets to track the requisite underlying data and administer the benefits. The VA OIG determined that approximately half of VA improper payments for housing allowances and book and supplies stipends may be related to inaccurate and/or incomplete information on Certs.[98]

The additional burden on SCOs to administer Post-9/11 GI Bill benefits is mirrored by the additional burden on FAAs to administer Pell Grants. IHEs often purchase or develop auxiliary software to support data entry into ED-funded software systems. ED has found that IHEs have difficulty reporting changes in student enrollment status accurately, measuring and monitoring satisfactory academic progress, and reporting in a timely manner.[99] Some IHE representatives have indicated that this student tracking and the subsequent calculation of the amount of aid to return is excessively complicated and burdensome.[100] This results in some students receiving HEA Title IV aid for which they are not eligible.

Both the GI Bill programs and Pell Grant program pay institutions a fee to defray the cost of the administrative burden based on the number of beneficiaries. It would be difficult for either federal agency to redevelop their systems to accommodate the variety of internal systems used by educational institutions, IHEs, and training establishments to track their own students and trainees. The VA and ED could provide a single interface or system and calculate benefits using the same information in order to reduce the institutional burden.

Inconsistent Automation of Supplemental Claims Systems and Delays in Disbursement of Funds

A long-standing complaint of Post-9/11 GI Bill participants and educational institutions regarding benefit administration is late payments.[101] A few months after initial implementation of the Post-9/11 GI Bill in October 2009, average processing time for initial applications and eligibility determinations (original claims) exceeded 59 days, and the average processing time for enrollments and payments (supplemental claims) exceeded 48 days.[102] The VA implemented several short-term solutions to increase the processing speed and continued implementation of its Long-Term Solution (LTS), an automated processing system. In FY2014, the average processing time was reduced to 17 days for initial claims and six days for supplemental claims.[103]

Payments have also been delayed as a result of inclement weather events affecting RPO operations, educational institutions and training establishments not submitting Certs in a timely manner, remarks entered in VA-ONCE that require manual follow-up by VCEs to resolve, and individuals not requesting benefits in a timely manner. In 2014, the VA Office of Inspector General (OIG) indicated that processing is delayed when Certs are submitted late (i.e., after the academic term begins).[104] The OIG recommended that processing speeds could be improved by educating veterans and SCOs on their responsibilities and having the RPO effectively monitor the timeliness of SCO submissions.[105] As a result of some payment delays, some educational institutions make special allowances for Post-9/11 GI Bill recipients for whom tuition and fees are not received by institutional deadlines, including short-term loans or extended deadlines. There is anecdotal evidence that some Post-9/11 GI Bill participants have had to change housing arrangements or withdraw from school as a result of delayed payments.

There are several options for expediting payments. While LTS and the remainder of the VA processing architecture automate many but not all of the required processes, additional automation and system integration could reduce processing times. For example, ED relies on a suite of automated and integrated systems, including COD, CPS, and NSLDS, to facilitate processing HEA Title IV aid. Automating the paper Certs may reduce the burden on individuals, educational institutions, and training establishments. In addition, the VA, State Approving Agencies (SAA), and VA Education Liaison Representatives (ELRs) could conduct or make available additional training and outreach to improve the accuracy and timeliness of Certs.

End of the Month Housing Allowance

Timing of the housing allowance payment has created issues for some individuals. Statutory provisions require that educational assistance benefits be paid only for periods of enrollment or pursuit unless an individual qualifies for an advance payment.[106] The first monthly housing allowance of an academic term is paid, at the earliest, after the term begins—typically at the beginning of the second month for the previous month's enrollment. Some individuals would like to receive the first housing allowance of the term before the term begins.

Pell Grant awards provide a lump sum payment up to 10 days prior to the start of the payment period that may, if adequate, be used to defray housing costs throughout the payment period. The Post-9/11 GI Bill could consider a similar lump sum payment prior to the start of the academic term; although, this would likely increase the incidence and amount of overpayments and debts.

Inconsistent Tuition and Fees Benefits

The possible variation in tuition and fees payment amounts from term to term for individuals attending private educational institutions may make personal financial management more difficult. Statutory provisions define the maximum annual tuition and fees benefit for individuals attending private educational institutions. The VA allows individuals attending private educational institutions to receive the maximum annual tuition and fees benefit in the first academic term of the academic year if eligible. Therefore, the tuition and fees benefit in subsequent terms of the same academic year may be lower or $0 unless the individual is eligible for a Yellow Ribbon payment. For example, if a student attending a private educational institution in academic year 2014-2015 is charged $12,000 tuition and fees for the fall term, $12,000 tuition and fees for the spring term, and $6,000 tuition and fees for the summer term, the student could receive Post-9/11 GI Bill tuition and fees benefits of up to $12,000 for the fall term, $8,235.02 for the spring term, and $0 for the summer term ($12,000 + $8,235.02 + $0 = $20,235.02, the academic year 2014- 2015 tuition and fees cap). The payment differences may affect recipient attendance decisions.

The Pell Grant disbursement methodology attempts to avoid this inconsistency by calculating a maximum award amount for the year and disbursing no more than a prorated amount based on the number of expected payment periods in the year. For example, an individual with a maximum award of $5,000 for the year will receive no more than $2,500 for the fall semester and $2,500 for the spring semester.[107] The Post-9/11 GI Bill tuition and fees at private and foreign institutions could follow a similar methodology to reduce the variation in amounts from term to term. There are, however, several potential issues that may arise with such a change. Pell Grant recipients do not receive the maximum award amount to which they are eligible for the year if they do not enroll in each of the expected payment periods. For example, in the above scenario, the student would not receive the remaining $2,500 of the $5,000 maximum if not enrolled in the spring semester. This change may reduce the perceived benefit of the Post-9/11 GI Bill and affect recipient's attendance decisions. In addition, the change may affect the cost of the Yellow Ribbon program.

Confusion and Adversity Regarding Overpayment and Debt Resolution

Complaints have arisen because educational institutions and Post-9/11 GI Bill participants believe that overpayments are erroneously assigned to them, and they have been unable to resolve overpayments or the ensuing debt with the least amount of difficulty or without adverse consequences. Specifically, both educational institutions and participants are unclear of the process required to resolve overpayments and debts. In addition, the process is perceived as being unnecessarily punitive. Reports indicate that this confusion has variously resulted in students dropping out of school to resolve overpayments, schools reassigning debt to students, and students' credit ratings being reduced.[108]

There are several options for diminishing confusion and adverse consequences. The VA could improve communication. For example, the VA could improve its explanation of the genesis of each overpayment and the steps for resolution. Although all of this information is included in the overpayment notification letters from the VA RPO and DMC, the text of the letters and timeline for action may not be comprehensible to all parties. The VA could make real-time information on the status of overpayments and the timeline for action easily accessible, and make their resolution available online regardless of whether the overpayment/debt resides with the RPO, DMC, or Treasury. Also along the lines of improved communication, the VA could provide VCEs with access to view the claimant's overpayment, debt, timeline for action, and terms of the debt resolution so that the VCEs could assist GI Bill participants with questions and issues. The VA could consider alternate forms of communication in addition to mail.

The VA and Congress could also change and/or clarify the process for mitigating adverse consequences.[109] For example, the VA could complete implementation of monthly enrollment certification by participants. In the event that SCOs do not notify the VA of enrollment changes in a timely manner, the participant would at the end of each month have the opportunity to inform the VA. This may reduce the amount of some overpayments.

Conversely, the VA could induce or penalize SCOs to encourage the timely amendment or adjustment to Certs. Another approach might be for the VA to begin immediate and minimal collection of overpayments from future benefits such that some individuals who choose not to proactively resolve an overpayment in a timely manner could avoid referral to Treasury and credit agencies. The minimal reduction might encourage individual action toward a more beneficial resolution of the overpayment. As an alternative to an automatic and minimal collection rate, the VA could automatically offset each future Post-9/11 GI Bill payment until the overpayment is resolved or the participant makes alternative arrangements. Finally, the RPO, DMC, and Treasury could improve system coordination or communication such that debtors are not penalized for remitting payments to the wrong entity. For example, a participant who sends a payment to the DMC after the debt has been referred to Treasury may be subject to Treasury action before the DMC, participant, and Treasury have an opportunity to appropriately apply the payment.

Issues related to assigning responsibility for HEA Title IV overpayments are not as prominent, but calculating the HEA Title IV debt amount is an issue. IHEs determine whether the student or IHE is responsible for the overpayment. If the student is responsible for a Pell Grant overpayment, the FAA will first attempt to resolve the overpayment through a reduction in subsequent disbursements in the same award year and then by contacting the student for repayment. However, the calculation and process by which IHEs complete a Return of Title IV Funds is a major source of concern for ED and IHEs. ED has determined that IHEs often make errors in calculating the amount of funds by using incorrect dates or making mathematical errors.[110] In addition, IHEs fail to follow ED regulations and IHE policy regarding the timeframe for returning funds. IHEs have requested a simplified process and more time to process returns.[111]

The adverse consequences of not resolving a GI Bill or Pell Grant overpayment within the specified timeframes are very similar: individuals lose eligibility for future benefits, debts are referred to the next agency organizational level (VA DMC or ED's Debt Resolution Services) and finally Treasury.

APPENDIX A. COMPARISON OF INSTITUTIONS OF HIGHER LEARNING AND INSTITUTIONS OF HIGHER EDUCATION

Table A-1. Institutions of Higher Learning and Institutions of Higher Education: Comparison of Select Attributes

Select Attributes	Institution of Higher Learning (IHL)	Institution of Higher Education (IHE)
Statutory definition citation	Title 38 U.S.C §3452(f)	Section 102 of the Higher Education Act
Control		
Public, private for-profit, private not-for-profit	Yes	Yes
Level		
Less than two-year postsecondary institutions Hospitals offering postsecondary educational programs Associate's degree granting institutions	NoYesYes	Yes Yes Yes
Bachelor's degree and above granting institutions	Yes	Yes
Additional Criteria		
Authorized by state or jurisdiction Accreditation by an ED-recognized accrediting entity	RequiredNot required	Required Required

Source: Table compiled by CRS based on statutory provisions.
Notes: Additional eligibility criteria apply.

APPENDIX B. ACRONYMS

Acronyms Related to the Post-9/11 GI Bill

Information Systems

BDN	the Benefits Delivery Network
BIRLS	Beneficiary Identification and Record Locator Subsystem

LTS	VA Long-Term Solution
PCGL	VA Personal Computer Generated Letters system
TIMS	The Imaging Management System (VA)
TINQ	Payment History Inquiry Screen
VA-ONCE	VA-Online Certification of Enrollment
VADIR	Veterans Affairs/Department of Defense Identity Repository
VID	Veteran Identification Data
VIS V	eterans Information Solution
VONAPP	Veterans' Online Application
WEAMS	VA Web Enabled Approval Management System

Programs

Ch. 33	Post-9/11 GI Bill
DEA	Survivors' and Dependents' Educational Assistance Program
Fry Scholarship	Post-9/11 GI Bill Marine Gunnery Sergeant John David Fry Scholarship Program
MGIB-AD	Montgomery GI Bill-Active Duty
MGIB-SR	Montgomery GI Bill-Selected Reserve
REAP	Reserve Educational Assistance Program
TA	DOD Tuition Assistance program
TOP	U.S. Department of Treasury Offset Program
VEAP	Post-Vietnam Era Veterans Educational Assistance Program
YR	Post-9/11 GI Bill Yellow Ribbon GI Education Enhancement Program

Other Acronyms

BAH	Basic Allowance for Housing
Cert	VA Certificate of Enrollment
COE	GI Bill Certificate of Eligibility
DMC	VA Debt Management Center
EFT	Electronic Funds Transfer (direct deposit)
ELR	VA Education Liaison Representative
IHL	Institution of Higher Learning
NCD	Non-college Degree Programs
NOI	VA Notice of Indebtedness
OJT	On the Job Training

RPOs	VA Regional Processing Offices
SCO	School Certifying Official
ToE	Transfer of Entitlement
VCE	Veterans Claims Examiner

Acronyms Related to the Pell Grant Program

Information Systems

COD	ED Common Origination and Disbursement
CPS	ED Central Processing System
EDE	Electronic Data Exchange
NSLDS	National Student Loan Data System

Other Acronyms

COA	HEA Title IV Cost of Attendance
EFC	HEA Title IV Expected Family Contribution
FAA	Financial Aid Administrator
FAFSA	Free Application for Federal Student Aid
HEA	Higher Education Act
HEA Title IV aid	Aid authorized by Title IV of the Higher Education Act
IASG	Iraq and Afghanistan Service Grant
IHE	Institutions of Higher Education
ISIR	ED Institutional Student Information Record
ROTC	Reserves Officers' Training Corps
SAR	ED Student Aid Report

APPENDIX C. POST-9/11 GI BILL SECONDARY PROCESSING AND DISBURSEMENT OF FUNDS FOR ADDITIONAL FORMS OF EDUCATION AND TRAINING

The administration of Post-9/11 GI Bill vocational flight training, apprenticeships or on-the-job training (OJT), tutorial assistance, correspondence training, licensing and certification tests, national tests, and relocation differs significantly from the administration of other degree and non-college degree (NCD) programs at educational institutions. The following explains the processes with respect to the secondary processing (supplemental claims) and disbursement of funds.

Certification of Flight Training

As part of the initial enrollment certification, the flight school must complete VA-ONCE or the applicable sections of the Certifications for VA Enrollment Certification (VA FORM 22-1999). This certification is used to indicate the student's eligibility for the flight training program and indicate the flight training plan. The form requires the individual's identifying information; name of program; certification that the student has a private pilot's license; certification that the student has a class I and/or II medical certificate on file at the school, as applicable; credit allowed for previous education and training; number of hours/units of instruction in current training plan; training dates; and charges.

Flight schools that are not institutions of higher learning (IHLs) must certify the number of training hours completed by each student monthly using VA-ONCE or the Monthly Certification of Flight Training (VA FORM 22-6553c). The form requires the individual's identifying information, course, type of instruction, applicable horsepower, hours, charge rate, total instructional charges, a summary of cumulative instruction, medical certification,[112] course completion or interruption, remarks, and the signatures of the student and SCO. Finally, the paper Cert is signed by the student and SCO and mailed to the appropriate RPO.

Certification of Apprenticeships or On-the-Job Training

Certs for pursuit of approved programs of apprenticeships or OJT are generally completed on paper and mailed or emailed to the relevant RPO. The Cert may be completed using VA Form 22- 1999, VA Enrollment Certification, or on letterhead of the training establishment. Apprenticeship and OJT Certs certify training completed in the previous month. The earliest the Cert can be submitted is the last calendar day of the month being certified. The Cert must identify the eligible individual, program of education, training dates, hours during which the individual was employed and training, and number of hours in a standard work week. Finally, the Cert must be signed by both the eligible individual and certifying official.

In addition, the Cert must be accompanied by a signed copy of the training agreement outlining the training program and wage scale. The training agreement may be completed using VA Form 22-8864, Training Agreement for Apprenticeship and Other On-The-Job Training Programs, or another comparable method. A training agreement describes the trainee, credit for previous training or experience, planned training period, wage progression, skills to be achieved and expected timing for achievement, and any required educational curriculum or training provided outside the job. The training agreement must be signed by the VA Education Liaison Representative (ELR), trainee, and a designated representative of the training establishment. The ELR acts as the liaison between the RPO and area educational institutions and training establishments, conducts some program approval functions, and ensures educational institutions and training establishments follow laws and policies.

Many individuals who pursue OJT or apprenticeship programs also enroll in NCD programs. For example, individuals pursuing permanent employment as police officers may attend a NCD program at a law enforcement academy and pursue OJT through a field training program.

Certification of Tutorial Assistance

An Application and Enrollment Certification for Individualized Tutorial Assistance (VA Form 22- 1990t) is used to certify tutorial assistance received in the previous month(s). The individual must need tutoring to pass a course in which he/she is currently enrolled and which is required for the approved program of education, and must be enrolled at least half-time in a postsecondary program. The Cert must be submitted no later than one year after the tutorial assistance. The form requires the individual's identifying information, credit hour load, educational objective, course that requires tutoring, tutor's identifying information, and tutoring schedule and charges. Finally, the Cert must be signed by the student, tutor, course professor or instructor, and SCO and mailed to the applicable RPO.

Certification of Correspondence Training

Correspondence training is certified by mail on VA Form 22-1999 (Enrollment Certification). The Cert requires the individual's identifying information; the type of training (flight, correspondence, or apprenticeship or other on-the-job training); the name of the approved program of education; the number of credits the student received for previous training; and the date and number of correspondence lessons sent to the student, including charges. The Cert must be signed by the SCO of the educational institution.

In addition, the Cert must be accompanied by a signed copy of the enrollment agreement affirming that the student has, upon reflection, determined that the course is suitable to the student's abilities and interests. The enrollment agreement is completed using VA Form 22-1999c, Certificate of Affirmation of Enrollment Agreement Correspondence Course. The enrollment agreement lists the trainee, course name, date agreement signed, educational institution, and credit for previous training or experience. The enrollment agreement must be signed by the student and mailed to the educational institution. The educational institution submits the enrollment agreement and Cert to the applicable RPO.

Certification of Pursuit by Eligible Individual

Reimbursement for licensing and certification tests, national tests, and relocation only requires certification by the eligible individual.

Licensing and Certification Tests

Eligible individuals who want to be reimbursed for approved licensing and certification tests must complete the Application for Reimbursement of Licensing or Certification Test (VA Form 22- 0803-ARE) or a self-prepared request for reimbursement. VA Form 22-0803 provides the individual identifying information; the applicable GI Bill program; the test name, date taken, and cost; and the organization that issues the applicable license or certificate. The eligible individual must sign and date the form or request. The form or request and either (1) a copy of the test results or (2) proof of payment and a copy of the license or certification must be received by the appropriate RPO within one year of taking the test.

National Tests

Eligible individuals who want reimbursement for approved national tests must submit a signed and dated request to the appropriate RPO. The request must provide individual identifying information; the test name, date taken, cost, and sponsoring organization; a copy of the test results; and, depending on the test, proof of payment.[113]

Relocation

Eligible individuals who want to be reimbursed for rural relocation expenses must complete the Application for Rural Relocation Benefit under the Post- 9/11 GI Bill (VA Form 22-0848). The form requires the individual's identifying information; current and prior addresses; the nature of the relocation; and proof of the rural address and air transportation, if applicable. The eligible individual must sign and date the form before mailing it to the appropriate RPO.

Processing of Certifications

Flight Certs for training that is not at an IHL are imaged into TIMS. The VCE re-verifies the claimant's eligibility as if issuing a COE and manually populates LTS and BDN. The VCE verifies that the claimant's medical certification is up to date in TIMS. The VCE also verifies that the program of education is approved and is being pursued in accordance with the WEAMS program requirements and VA-FORM-1999 training plan. For example, the VCE must ensure that individuals are not paid for flight training hours that exceed those required for the program. The program approval in WEAMS is captured in TIMS. Finally, the VCE reviews prior flight training Certs to ensure the current training is not duplicative. The VCE calculates the payment amounts.

Apprenticeship, OJT, and correspondence training agreements and Certs are imaged into TIMS. The VCE re-verifies the claimant's eligibility as if issuing a COE and manually populates LTS and BDN.[114] The VCE verifies that the program of education is approved in WEAMS and COOL (a database of apprenticeship and OJT providers, including employer information, the SCO's identifying information, program descriptions, journeyman rates, planned hours, and program length) and is being pursued in accordance with the training agreement, including wage levels and program length. The program approval in WEAMS or COOL is captured in TIMS. LTS calculates the books and supplies and housing stipends automatically, primarily based on the number of certified hours, but the VCE may be required to make adjustments and manually calculate the amounts. A monthly housing benefit is paid for completed and certified training. The books and supplies stipend is paid as a lump-sum for upcoming training. For individuals who do not complete their program, a portion of the books and supplies stipend may become an overpayment (see Overpayments section), but the housing stipend will not.

Licensing, certification, and national test Certs are imaged into TIMS. The VCE re-verifies the claimant's eligibility as if issuing a COE and manually populates LTS and BDN. The VCE verifies that the program of education is approved and for what amount in WEAMS and COOL. Finding licensing and certification tests in WEAMS involves a cumbersome text search by VCEs, especially since some test names may not be uniformly referenced. The test approval in WEAMS or COOL is captured in TIMS. If the test is not approved, the VCE sends the claimant a denial letter that may advise the claimant to contact the SAA to gain approval. The VCE also ensures that the claimant has sufficient entitlement remaining. Payments are generally made within two to three days of VCE authorization.

End Notes

[1] "GI Bill" is a federally registered trademark owned by the Department of Veterans Affairs (VA).

[2] See, for example: U.S. Congress, House Committee on Veterans' Affairs, Subcommittee on Economic Opportunity, *A Review of Higher Education Opportunities for the Newest Generation of Veterans*, 114th Cong., 1st sess., March 17, 2015; U.S. Congress, House Committee on Veterans' Affairs, Subcommittee on Economic Opportunity, *Increasing the Functionality of Post 9/11 GI Bill Claims Processing to Reduce Delays*, 113th Cong., 1st sess., February 14, 2013; U.S. Congress, House Committee on Veterans' Affairs, Subcommittee on Economic Opportunity, *Update of the Post-9/11 GI Bill*, 111th Cong., 2nd sess., September 16, 2010.

[3] For more information on the GI Bills, see CRS Report R42785, *GI Bills Enacted Prior to 2008 and Related Veterans' Educational Assistance Programs: A Primer*, by Cassandria Dortch.

[4] FY2016 President's budget request.

[5] The uniformed services include the Army, Navy, Marine Corps, Air Force, and Coast Guard, including the reserve components, and commissioned officers of the Public Health Service (PHS) and the National Oceanic Atmospheric Association (NOAA).

[6] These requirements and process for approving programs of education are outside the scope of this report.

[7] P.L. 110-252.

[8] In cases in which tuition and fees charged by an institution of higher learning (IHL) are not fully covered by the tuition and fees payment benefits, the IHL may voluntarily enter into a Yellow Ribbon Program agreement with the VA to match an equal percentage of some portion of the remaining tuition and fees.

[9] Statutory provisions provide some exceptions to these periods of benefit availability.

[10] FY2015 President's budget request.

[11] CRS analysis of 2012-2013 data from the U.S. Department of Veterans Affairs, Congressional Liaison, emailed to CRS on February 25, 2014.

[12] VR&E is an entitlement program that provides job training and related services to veterans with service-connected disabilities. For more information, see CRS Report RL34627, *Veterans' Benefits: The Vocational Rehabilitation and Employment Program*, by Benjamin Collins.

[13] For more information on Stafford Loans, see CRS Report R40122, *Federal Student Loans Made Under the Federal Family Education Loan Program and the William D. Ford Federal Direct Loan Program: Terms and Conditions for Borrowers*, by David P. Smole. For more information on Federal Supplemental Educational Opportunity Grants (FSEOG), Federal Perkins Loans, and Federal Work-Study programs, see CRS Report RL31618, *Campus-Based Student Financial Aid Programs Under the Higher Education Act*, by Alexandra Hegji and David P. Smole.

[14] U.S. Department of Education, Office of Federal Student Aid, *Federal Student Aid Annual Report FY2014*, November 14, 2014.

[15] P.L. 89-329.

[16] The Pell Grant award year begins the first day of July in a given year and ends the last day of June the following year.

[17] Students who first enroll on or after July 1, 2012, must have a high school diploma, the recognized equivalent, or have completed homeschooling at the secondary level. Students who enrolled prior to July 1, 2012, and do not have a high school diploma or recognized equivalent, must either (1) demonstrate an ability to benefit from postsecondary education by passing an examination approved by ED to be eligible for federal student aid, or (2) successfully complete six credits or 225 clock hours of college work applicable to a certificate or degree offered by a postsecondary institution.

[18] Students must generally be U.S. citizens, U.S. nationals, U.S. permanent residents, eligible noncitizens, or citizens of the Freely Associated States.

[19] Non-exempt males between 18 and 25 years of age must have registered with the Selective Service System (SSS).

[20] Conviction for possession or sale of drugs while receiving federal student aid may disqualify students. A federal or state judge may deny persons convicted of drug trafficking or possession from receiving student aid. The student can regain eligibility by waiting out the ineligibility period, completing a rehabilitation program, having the conviction removed, or passing two unannounced drug tests. Students are ineligible if they have failed to resolve a default on a Title IV student loan, have inadvertently exceeded annual or aggregate Title IV loan limits, have failed to repay or make arrangements to repay an overpayment on Title IV aid, have failed to repay Title IV funds obtained fraudulently, or are subject to a judgment lien for a debt owed to the United States. Students who are incarcerated in a federal or state penal institution are ineligible for Pell Grants. Students who are subject to an involuntary civil commitment following incarceration for a sexual offense (as determined under the Federal Bureau of Investigation's (FBI's) Uniform Crime Reporting (UCR) Program) are ineligible. A default on a Title IV student loan may be resolved through repayment in full;

six consecutive, full, voluntary, and on-time payments under an approved repayment arrangement; or loan rehabilitation through nine consecutive, full, voluntary, and on-time payments within 10 consecutive months under an approved repayment arrangement. In addition, individuals who have earned a bachelor's degree, more advanced degree, or the equivalent are ineligible for Pell Grants.

[21] For more information on eligible IHEs, see CRS Report R43159, *Institutional Eligibility for Participation in Title IV Student Financial Aid Programs*, by Alexandra Hegji.

[22] The requirements and process for determining eligible programs are outside the scope of this report.

[23] A remedial course is a course of study designed to increase the ability of a student to pursue a course of study leading to a certificate or degree. A remedial course is not preparatory coursework, which prepares a student for a given program.

[24] Correspondence or "home study" courses provide instructional materials and exams to students who do not physically attend classes at the school and who are studying independently. Exams are returned to the school for grading. If the course uses video cassettes or discs and the school provides the same instruction to students who physically attend classes, the course is not considered correspondence.

[25] FAFSA is a registered trademark of Federal Student Aid, U.S. Department of Education.

[26] CRS analysis of 2011-2012 data from the U.S. Department of Education, Integrated Postsecondary Education Data System (IPEDS).

[27] The Higher Education Amendments of 1998 (1998 Amendments; P.L. 105-244) required the Department of Education to develop a plan for a modernized system for the delivery of HEA Title IV aid programs, including an open, common, and integrated delivery and information system.

[28] U.S. Government Accountability Office, *Veterans' Disability Benefits: Challenges to Timely Processing Persist*, GAO-13-453T, March 13, 2013.

[29] U.S. Department of Education, *2012-2013 Federal Pell Grant Program End-of-Year Report*, Table 1.

[30] As of January 2014, the VA was processing original claims in an average of less than 20 days according to the Department of Veterans Affairs, "Automation Speeds Benefits Processing for Post-9/11 GI Bill Students," press release, January 29, 2014.

[31] CPS is operated, maintained, and managed by an ED contractor.

[32] The forms are available on the VA's website or in a VA office.

[33] 38 U.S.C. §§5110 and 5113.

[34] The DOD transfer process is outside the scope of this report.

[35] Despite the irrevocable election, individuals may choose to receive payments as if under the relinquished program.

[36] FY2015 President's budget request.

[37] U.S. Congress, House Committee on Veterans' Affairs, Subcommittee on Economic Opportunity, *Increasing the Functionality of Post-9/11 GI Bill Claims Processing to Reduce Delays*, 113th Cong., 1st sess., February 14, 2013, Serial No. 113-4.

[38] U.S. Department of Veterans Affairs, *2014 Performance and Accountability Report*, 2014, p. Part II-40.

[39] See the discussion beginning on page II-169 of http://www.va.gov/budget/docs/report/PartII/2011- VAPAR_Part_II.pdf, in which the VA notes issues updating its IT processing and payment system to keep up with congressional changes to the Post-9/11 GI Bill; and U.S. Department of Veterans Affairs, *2014 Performance and Accountability Report*, 2014, p. Part II-40.

[40] Alternative calculation procedures are applied if students are expected to enroll for less than or more than nine months during the award year.

[41] The family income threshold is established in statutory provisions and has not been changed since at least the 1998 reauthorization of HEA. For tax filers, this threshold is based on the adjusted gross income (AGI) amount. For non-taxfilers, the threshold is based on earned income.

[42] The applicable means-tested federal benefit programs are the Supplemental Security Income (SSI) Program, the Supplemental Nutrition Assistance Program (SNAP), the Free and Reduced Price School Lunch Program, the Temporary Assistance for Needy Families (TANF) Program, and the Special Supplemental Nutrition Program for Women, Infants, and Children (WIC).

[43] A dislocated worker is defined in Section 101(9) of the Workforce Investment Act (WIA) as a "displaced worker."

[44] For tax filers, this threshold is based on the adjusted gross income (AGI) amount. For non-tax filers, the threshold is based on earned income.

[45] The maximum family income level is specified in statutory provisions and adjusted according to increases in the Consumer Price Index (CPI).

[46] The award is termed an Iraq and Afghanistan Service Grant (IASG), and the zero EFC applies only to calculating the Pell Grant amount, not other HEA Title IV aid.

[47] A sample SAR is available at http://ifap.ed.gov/eannouncements/attachments/021114SAR EnglishMockUp.pdf.

[48] Non-college degree refers to programs that do not lead to a postsecondary degree. Non-college degree programs include diplomas and certificate programs.

[49] Resident training includes conventional classroom sessions and other coursework such as a doctoral dissertation or student teaching. For more information see 38 C.F.R. 21.4267(d).

[50] Out-of-state charges are only reported if the student is charged as an out-of state student and the school is contributing toward the difference between in-state and out-of-state charges through the Yellow Ribbon program.

[51] VA educational benefits cannot be paid to non-matriculated college or university students unless they are pending admission or are pursuing a degree at another college or university. The VA defines matriculated as having been formally admitted to a college or university. Students pending admission may be certified for two quarters or semesters.

[52] Under DOD Tuition Assistance (TA), military service branches may pay a certain amount of tuition and expenses for the education and training of active duty personnel and members of the Selected Reserve. In general, the individual submits an approved TA authorization or request to the educational institution. The educational institution processes the authorization and receives payment from the service branch. TA and Post-9/11 GI Bill benefits cannot be used for the same course.

[53] Statutory provisions except Pell Grants, but VA guidance may include all forms of Title IV aid.

[54] The SCO must maintain a record in the individual's student file verifying the courses that satisfy the requirements of the chosen program of education. In the final academic year, the individual may enroll in and be certified for additional courses in order to maintain full-time enrollment status.

[55] Documentation of the need for remedial or deficiency courses must be maintained in the individual's student file.

[56] Multiple terms may be certified if the total duration adds to 15 weeks.

[57] The rate of pursuit is the number of credits (or equivalents) pursued divided by the number of credits considered full-time by the institution (or 18 clock hours if classroom instruction predominates and 22 clock hours if shop practice predominates).

[58] See Appendix A for a description of IHLs.

[59] The IHL matches the YR payment.

[60] Some individuals may be eligible for supplemental assistance (Kickers) of up to $950 per month based on their military service branch agreement.

[61] Data provided by the VA to CRS in email dated December 24, 2014.

[62] U.S. Department of Veterans Affairs, *2014 Performance and Accountability Report*, 2014, p. Part II-40.

[63] Statistics calculated by CRS based on data emailed to CRS from the VA Office of Congressional and Legislative Affairs on November 21, 2011.

[64] In academic year 2012-2013, approximately 45% of Pell Grant eligible applicants were selected for verification; U.S. Department of Education, *2012-2013 Federal Pell Grant Program End-of-Year Report*, Table 1.

[65] In accordance with Section 478 of the HEA, the Secretary does not have the authority to prescribe regulations regarding COA.

[66] The COA includes an allowance to cover the basic expenses incurred only for board for students living in housing provided on a military base or for which a basic living allowance is provided.

[67] The maximum award is the sum of a discretionary maximum award specified in annual appropriations acts and a mandatory add-on amount specified in the law.

[68] The statutory minimum may differ from the actual minimum due to ED calculation methodology.

[69] The Veterans' Work-Study allowance is included in income used to calculate EFC.

[70] HEA specifies requirements for entrance counseling for borrowers but does not specify counseling requirements for non-borrowers.

[71] The requirements for disbursing Pell Grant funds differ for correspondence programs.

[72] For more information on the methods for schools to receive HEA Title IV funds, see U.S. Department of Education, *Common Origination and Disbursement 2015-2016 Technical Reference*, Volume VI, Section 2, http://www.ifap.ed.gov/codtechref/attachments/1516CODTechRefVol6Sec2FundingMethods.pdf.

[73] In the event that an IHE was unable to disburse the funds within three days for reasons outside the IHE's control, the IHE may retain for up to seven days an amount of excess cash that does not exceed 1% of the total amount of funds the school drew down in the prior award year.

[74] U.S Department of Education, Office of Postsecondary Education, *2011-2012 Federal Pell Grant Program End-ofYear Report*, Table 18.

[75] Individuals who choose to change GI Bills must submit a new application.

[76] VA Form 22-1995 (Request for Change of Program or Place of Training) or VA Form 22-5495 (Dependents' Request for Change of Program or Place of Training).

[77] The student must either regain satisfactory academic progress by the end of one payment period, or the student must make progress and meet satisfactory academic progress according to an IHE-developed academic plan.

[78] For more information on TOP, see CRS Report RL34660, *Federal Government Debt Collection: An Overview of the Treasury Offset and Federal Payment Levy Programs*, by Gary Guenther.

[79] The Committee on Waivers and Compromises (COWC) at each RPO has the authority to consider waiver of all student benefit overpayments.

[80] 38 C.F.R. §1.911(d)(4); 38 C.F.R. §1.912a; and U.S. Department of Veterans Affairs, FAQs, *What steps does VA take to collect a debt under any GI Bill education program?*, updated September 29, 2014.

[81] U.S. Department of Veterans Affairs, *2013 Performance and Accountability Report*, pp. IV-14.

[82] Regulations limit the amount a student must return to the amount by which the original overpayment exceeds 50% of the total grant funds disbursed or could have been disbursed to the student for the payment period or period of enrollment and limit the amount due from a student to the amount by which the original grant overpayment exceeds 50% of the total Title IV grant funds disbursed or could have been disbursed to the student.

[83] U.S. Government Accountability Office, *Veterans' Education Benefits: Enhanced Guidance and Collaboration Could Improve Administration of the Post-9/11 GI Bill Program*, GAO-11-356R, May 5, 2011.

[84] P.L. 110-315.

[85] U.S. Congress, House Committee on Veterans' Affairs, *Amending Title 38, United States Code, To Direct the Secretary of Veterans Affairs to Develop a Comprehensive Policy to Improve Outreach and Transparency to Veterans and Members of the Armed Forces Through the Provision of Information on Institutions of Higher Learning, and for Other Purposes*, To accompany H.R. 4057, 112th Cong., 2nd sess., September 10, 2012.

[86] For examples, see U.S. Congress, House Committee on Veterans' Affairs, Subcommittee on Economic Opportunity, *Defining and Improving Success for Student Veterans*, Witness Testimony of Mr. Michael Dakduk, Vice President of Military and Veterans Affairs, Association of Private Sector Colleges and Universities (APSCU), 114th Cong., 2nd sess., May 8, 2014; or Kelley Holland, "Veterans face another battle: Paying for college," *CNBC*, November 20, 2014.

[87] P.L. 110-315 and U.S. Congress, House Committee on Education and Labor, College Opportunity and Affordability Act of 2007, to accompany H.R. 4137, 110th Cong., 1st sess., December 19, 2007, H.Rept. 110-500.

[88] http://www.gibill.va.gov/resources/benefits_resources/benefit_comparison_tools.html.

[89] U.S. Department of Veterans Affairs, Office of Inspector General, *Veterans Benefits Administration: Audit of Post-9/11 G.I. Bill Monthly Housing Allowance and Book Stipend Payments*, 13-01452-214, July 11, 2014.

[90] U.S. Congress, House Committee on Veterans' Affairs, Subcommittee on Economic Opportunity, *Increasing the Functionality of Post-9/11 GI Bill Claims Processing to Reduce Delays*, 113th Cong., 1st sess., February 14, 2013, Serial No. 113-4.

[91] Difficulties obtaining service records for members of the reserves and National Guard affect their access to other VA benefits. "Military records of National Guard or Reserve members can often be difficult to obtain, in particular, because these servicemembers typically have multiple, non-consecutive deployments with different units and their records may not always be held with their reserve units and may exist in multiple places"; According to U.S. Government Accountability Office, *Veterans' Disability Benefits: Challenges to Timely Processing Persist*, GAO-13-453T, March 13, 2013, p. 10.

[92] U.S. Congress, House Committee on Veterans' Affairs, Subcommittee on Economic Opportunity, *Increasing the Functionality of Post-9/11 GI Bill Claims Processing to Reduce Delays*, 113th Cong., 1st sess., February 14, 2013, Serial No. 113-4.

[93] U.S. Congress, House Committee on Veterans' Affairs, *Veterans Economic Opportunity Act of 2013*, Report to accompany H.R. 2481, 113th Cong., 1st sess., September 11, 2013, H.Rept. 113-207.

[94] U.S. Department of Veterans Affairs, Office of Inspector General, *Veterans Benefits Administration: Audit of Post-9/11 G.I. Bill Monthly Housing Allowance and Book Stipend Payments*, 13-01452-214, July 11, 2014.

[95] U.S. Department of Veterans Affairs, Office of Inspector General, *Veterans Benefits Administration: Audit of Post-9/11 G.I. Bill Monthly Housing Allowance and Book Stipend Payments*, 13-01452-214, July 11, 2014.

[96] Effie Barnett, Jan Brandow, U.S. Department of Education, "Top 10 Audit & Program Review Findings," Federal Student Aid Conference 2012, November 2012.

[97] U.S. Department of Education, *2012-2013 Federal Pell Grant Program End-of-Year Report*, Table 1; and Effie Barnett, Cassandra Weems, "Program Review Essentials and Top 10 Compliance Findings," U.S. Department of Education, 2014 FSA Training Conference for Financial Aid Professionals, December 2014.

[98] U.S. Department of Veterans Affairs, Office of Inspector General, *Veterans Benefits Administration: Audit of Post-9/11 G.I. Bill Monthly Housing Allowance and Book Stipend Payments*, 13-01452-214, July 11, 2014.

[99] Effie Barnett, Cassandra Weems, "Program Review Essentials and Top 10 Compliance Findings," U.S. Department of Education, 2014 FSA Training Conference for Financial Aid Professionals, December 2014.

[100] U.S. Government Accountability Office, *Higher Education: Experts Cited a Range of Requirements as Burdensome*, GAO-13-371, April 10, 2013, pp. 7-10.

[101] For example, see U.S. Congress, House Committee on Veterans' Affairs, Subcommittee on Economic Opportunity, *Increasing the Functionality of Post-9/11 GI Bill Claims Processing to Reduce Delays*, 114th Cong., 1st sess., February 14, 2013.

[102] VA Office of Inspector General, *Veterans Benefits Administration: Audit of Education Claims and Payments for the Post-9/11 GI Bill*, 09-03458-18, November 3, 2010.

[103] U.S. Department of Veterans Affairs, "Automation Speeds Benefits Processing for Post-9/11 GI Bill Students," press release, January 29, 2014.

[104] U.S. Department of Veterans Affairs, *2014 Performance and Accountability Report*, November 17, 2014.

[105] Department of Veterans Affairs, Office of Inspector General, *Veterans Benefits Administration: Audit of Post-9/11 G.I. Bill Monthly Housing Allowance and Books Stipend Payments*, 13-01452-214, July 11, 2014.

[106] 38 U.S.C. §3680.

[107] This example is a simplification of Pell Grant disbursement rules such that the amounts are subject to change based on the student's enrollment rate, cost of attendance, expected family contribution, and other factors.

[108] U.S. Congress, Senate Committee on Veterans' Affairs, *Hearing on Pending Benefits Legislation*, 113th Cong., 1st sess., June 12, 2013, S.Hrg. 113-111 (Washington: GPO, 2014), p. 175.

[109] U.S. Department of Veterans Affairs, Office of Inspector General, *Veterans Benefits Administration: Audit of Post-9/11 G.I. Bill Monthly Housing Allowance and Book Stipend Payments*, 13-01452-214, July 11, 2014.

[110] Effie Barnett, Cassandra Weems, "Program Review Essentials and Top 10 Compliance Findings," U.S. Department of Education, 2014 FSA Training Conference for Financial Aid Professionals, December 2014.

[111] American Council on Education, *Recalibrating Regulation of Colleges and Universities*, Report by the Task Force on Federal Regulation of Higher Education, February 12, 2015, pp. 19-20, 43-44.

[112] The individual must have the appropriate medical certification to be eligible for GI Bill benefits for flight training.

[113] An individual may submit the Statement in Support of Claim (VA Form 21-4138) with the supporting documentation.

[114] An individual cannot be certified for concurrent IHL and apprenticeship/OJT training.

In: The Post-9/11 GI Bill
Editor: Delores Norton

ISBN: 978-1-63485-161-9

Chapter 2

POST-9/11 GI BILL: ADDITIONAL ACTIONS NEEDED TO HELP REDUCE OVERPAYMENTS AND INCREASE COLLECTIONS*

United States Government Accountability Office

ABBREVIATIONS

OMB	Office of Management and Budget
Post-9/11 GI Bill	Post-9/11 Veterans Educational Assistance Act of 2008
VA	Department of Veterans Affairs
Yellow Ribbon Program	Yellow Ribbon G.I. Education Enhancement Program

WHY GAO DID THIS STUDY

VA provided $10.8 billion in Post-9/11 GI Bill education benefits to almost 800,000 veterans in fiscal year 2014. GAO was asked to review overpayments for the program, which can create financial hardships for

* This is an edited, reformatted and augmented version of The United States Government Accountability Office publication, GAO-16-42, dated October 2015.

veterans who are generally required to pay them back and which can result in a significant loss of taxpayer dollars if they are not collected.

This report examines (1) the extent of overpayments, (2) how effectively VA has addressed their causes, and (3) the effectiveness of VA's collection efforts. GAO analyzed overpayment data for fiscal years 2013 and 2014, examined the causes from a generalizable sample of high-dollar overpayments (greater than $1,667), conducted a case file review of 20 overpayments (selected for a variety of causes), and reviewed VA's monitoring of overpayments. GAO also interviewed senior and frontline staff at two VA offices that process claims and collect debts, officials at nine schools (selected for variation in program length and their status as public, nonprofit, and for-profit), higher education associations, and veteran service organizations.

WHAT GAO RECOMMENDS

Congress should consider granting VA explicit authority to require training for school officials. In addition, GAO is making a number of recommendations to improve VA's guidance and processes, including providing program guidance to veterans, verifying veterans' monthly enrollment, and developing additional debt notification methods. VA agreed with GAO's recommendations to the agency and plans to address these issues.

WHAT GAO FOUND

The Department of Veterans Affairs (VA) identified $416 million in Post-9/11 GI Bill overpayments in fiscal year 2014, affecting approximately one in four veteran beneficiaries and about 6,000 schools. Overpayments most often occur when VA pays benefits based on a student's enrollment at the beginning of the school term and the student later drops one or more classes (or withdraws from school altogether). Students therefore receive benefits for classes they did not complete, and the "overpayment" must be paid back to VA. A small percentage of overpayments occurred because of school reporting or VA processing errors. GAO found that most overpayments were collected quickly, but as of November 2014 (when VA provided these data to GAO), VA was still collecting $152 million in overpayments from fiscal year 2014, and an additional $110 million from prior years, primarily owed by veterans with the remainder owed by schools.

Inadequate guidance, processes, and training have limited VA's efforts to reduce overpayments caused by enrollment changes and school errors.

- *Guidance for veterans.* Many veterans may not realize they can incur overpayments as a result of enrollment changes because VA provides limited guidance to veterans on its policies. As a result, veterans may be unaware of the consequences of enrollment changes until after they have already incurred their first overpayment debt, according to school officials. Because VA is not effectively communicating its program policies to veterans, some veterans may be incurring debts that they could have otherwise avoided.
- *Enrollment verification process.* While veterans using other VA education programs have to verify their enrollment each month, VA generally does not require those using the Post-9/11 GI Bill to do so. By not requiring veterans to verify their enrollment every month, which can cause significant time to lapse between when veterans drop courses and when this is reported, VA's process allows veterans to incur thousands of dollars in overpayments and also increases the program's costs associated with collecting these debts.
- *Training for school officials.* Overpayments also occur when schools make errors, such as reporting enrollment information incorrectly, which VA officials said is sometimes attributable to a lack of training. For example, some school officials routinely made systematic errors reporting enrollment information, creating thousands of dollars in overpayments. Not all school officials attend the different training opportunities VA offers and VA officials said the agency lacks the authority to require school officials to participate in any of them. VA officials said they would like school officials to take a minimum level of training, which could help reduce errors and related overpayments.

The effectiveness of VA's collection efforts is hindered by its notification methods. VA relies solely on paper mail to notify schools and veterans of overpayments. VA generally sends veterans' notices to the addresses from veterans' initial benefit applications. However, these addresses can often be out-of-date, so some veterans do not receive the letters, leaving them unaware of their debts. This can cause veterans to unknowingly miss deadlines for disputing their debts and leave them unprepared to cover living expenses if

VA begins withholding future benefit payments or offsetting tax returns for collection. This can also lead to delays in the collection of overpayments from veterans.

* * *

October 21, 2015

The Honorable Thomas R. Carper
Ranking Member
Committee on Homeland Security and Governmental Affairs
United States Senate

Dear Senator Carper:

The Department of Veterans Affairs (VA) provided $10.8 billion in Post-9/11 GI Bill education benefits to almost 800,000 veterans and other beneficiaries in fiscal year 2014.[1] For eligible veterans, VA sends tuition and fee payments to schools, as well as housing benefits and book payments directly to the veteran, based on the initial enrollment information that schools submit to VA at the beginning of each term. If veterans subsequently reduce their course load (or withdraw from school altogether), it can reduce their eligible benefit amount, and any "overpayments" of tuition or housing benefits must be paid back to VA. Given the size and projected future growth of the Post-9/11 GI Bill program, these overpayments can result in a significant loss of taxpayer dollars if they are not recovered. In addition, overpayment debts can create financial hardships for veterans and administrative burdens for schools.

You asked us to review issues related to Post-9/11 GI Bill overpayments. This report examines:

1. What is known about the extent of Post-9/11 GI Bill overpayments and collections, and how effectively VA monitors them?
2. How effectively has VA addressed the causes of overpayments?
3. How effectively do VA's policies and procedures support the collection of overpayments?

To examine the extent of overpayments, we reviewed available Post-9/11 GI Bill financial data from fiscal years 2013 and 2014. We also analyzed data on all outstanding overpayment debts dating back to the start of the Post-9/11 GI Bill program in 2009. We assessed the reliability of these data by reviewing VA's reporting systems and conducting electronic testing of the underlying data, and we determined that the data were sufficiently reliable for our reporting purposes. We also reviewed VA's monitoring of overpayments and collections by examining its data tracking and reporting practices and assessed these efforts against guidance for government receivables in OMB Circular A-129.[2] To identify the causes of overpayments, we reviewed VA's Quarterly High-Dollar Overpayment Reports and supporting documentation for fiscal years 2013 and 2014. We assessed the reliability of these data through an in-depth file review of 20 overpayment cases and interviews with knowledgeable agency officials and we determined that the data were sufficiently reliable for our reporting purposes. We also reviewed a selection of school compliance surveys, which VA uses to assess whether schools that receive VA education benefits adhere to applicable laws and regulations. To examine the effectiveness of VA's efforts to address both the causes of overpayments and the collection of overpayment debts, we reviewed relevant federal laws, regulations, and policy guidance for processing and collecting VA debts. We interviewed senior VA officials and visited one of VA's four Regional Processing Offices as well as VA's debt collection office, the Debt Management Center, to interview management and frontline staff. We also interviewed representatives from several veterans service organizations, higher education associations, and administrators at nine schools about the effects of overpayments on veterans and schools. We selected the nine schools to include a mix of program lengths (2-year and 4-year schools), sectors (public, nonprofit, and for-profit), and student veteran populations ranging from 14 to more than 14,000. We assessed VA's efforts to address the causes of overpayments and collect overpayment debts against the requirements in the Post-9/11 GI Bill's statute and regulations, and government standards for internal controls. For more information on our scope and methodologies, see appendix I.

We conducted this performance audit from April 2014 to October 2015 in accordance with generally accepted government auditing standards. Those standards require that we plan and perform the audit to obtain sufficient, appropriate evidence to provide a reasonable basis for our findings and conclusions based on our audit objectives. We believe that the evidence obtained provides a reasonable basis for our findings and conclusions based on our audit objectives.

Background

Post-9/11 GI Bill Benefits

The Post-9/11 GI Bill, which took effect on August 1, 2009, is now VA's largest educational program.[3] In fiscal year 2014, the Post-9/11 GI Bill program had 790,000 participants and made $10.8 billion in payments for tuition, fees, housing, and books. This program provides benefits generally to veterans who served on active duty for at least 90 days on or after September 11, 2001.[4] Full benefits are available to those who served on active duty for 36 months, for which VA will pay the full in-state tuition and fees at any public school and up to an annual maximum amount at nonprofit and for-profit schools ($21,085 in academic year 2015-16).[5]

VA pays schools directly for tuition and fees and sends additional payments for housing and books directly to veterans who are eligible for these payments.[6] Housing benefits are provided to veterans through a monthly housing allowance, paid at the beginning of each month based on the previous month's enrollment, and the amount depends on the veteran's rate of academic pursuit (e.g., full- or part-time) and the geographic location of the school they are attending.[7]

For veterans to start receiving Post-9/11 GI Bill benefits, school employees, known as school certifying officials, must certify to VA that they are enrolled in classes (see fig. 1).[8] VA recommends that schools certify veteran enrollments prior to the start of the school term.

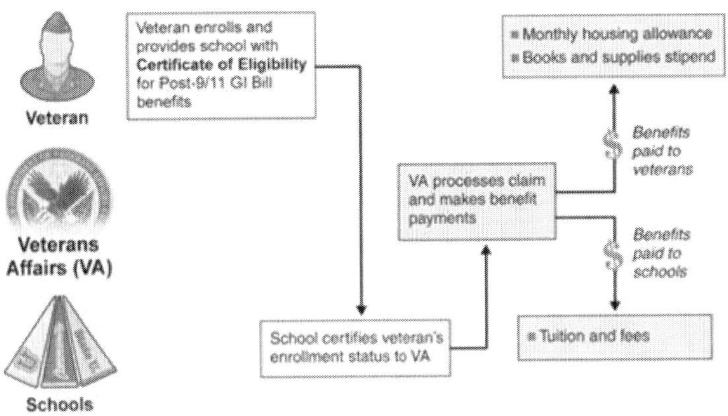

Source: GAO analysis of VA documents: GAO (images). | GAO-16-42.

Figure 1. VA's Processing of Post-9/11 GI Bill Payments.

Post-9/11 GI Bill Overpayments

Post-9/11 GI Bill overpayments occur when VA makes a payment in excess of what a veteran is entitled to. This can result from either erroneous payments or subsequent changes in the veteran's enrollment status or tuition or fee amounts after benefits have already been paid. Enrollment changes cause overpayments because the Post-9/11 GI Bill program, by design, pays tuition to schools in advance based on individual veterans' expected enrollment. These types of overpayments are not considered "improper" (i.e., made in error) because the payments were originally correct when issued.[9] Once VA begins paying Post-9/11 GI Bill benefits, veterans and schools are responsible for notifying VA of any changes in the veteran's enrollment (e.g., dropping a class or withdrawing from school) and schools are responsible for notifying VA of any subsequent adjustments in tuition or fees. VA processes these changes, which can increase or decrease the payment amounts veterans are eligible for. When enrollment changes decrease a veteran's calculated benefit amount, an overpayment is created for any excess funds VA has already paid. For example, tuition and fee overpayments can be created for any tuition and fees paid for classes that a veteran did not complete.[10] Changes in a veteran's enrollment can also affect the amount of housing and book stipend payments that the veteran is eligible to receive.

VA sends tuition and fee payments directly to schools on behalf of students, and VA often holds veterans liable for tuition and fee overpayments in accordance with its statutory authority.[11] Veterans are generally responsible for repaying any overpayments resulting from enrollment changes during the school term (see table 1).[12] Schools are only responsible for repaying these benefits to VA in certain circumstances, such as when the veteran completely withdraws from the school on or before the first day of the term.[13] Veterans are solely responsible for repaying any overpayments of housing or book stipend benefits. VA does not hold veterans liable for overpayments that result from administrative errors or an error in judgment on the part of VA, unless the veteran should have known the overpayment was patently excessive (such as a duplicate payment or a payment amount that exceeds the amount displayed on an award letter), according to VA officials.[14]

VA determines the type and amount of any overpayments based on the enrollment and tuition information submitted by schools or after identifying and correcting any school reporting or internal processing errors.

Table 1. Responsibility for Repaying Post-9/11 GI Bill Overpayment Debts

Schools are responsible for tuition overpayments when:	Veterans are responsible for tuition overpayments when:
•Student never attended any classes •Student completely withdraws on or before the first day of the term •Student died during the term or before start of the term[a] •School reports reduced tuition and fee charges and/or Yellow Ribbon amount[b] •School received an erroneous or duplicate payment from VA •Overpayment resulted from school's willful or negligent false certification or failure to certify significant changes	•Student withdrew after the first day of the term •Student reduced hours either before or during the term •Student attended at least one day of any of the certified classes •School reports a reduction in tuition, fees, and/or Yellow Ribbon amount dueto student action •Student drops a course and adds a course which results in a reduction in tuition, fees, and/or Yellow Ribbon amount, even if there is no net change in training time
	Veterans are also responsible for all housing and book stipend overpayments

Source: GAO analysis of VA guidance. | GAO-16-42.

[a] 38 C.F.R. § 21.9635(a).

[b] The Yellow Ribbon G.I, Education Enhancement (Yellow Ribbon) Program provides veterans attending participating private schools or public schools as out-of-state students with additional benefits to cover costs that exceed their Post-9/11 GI Bill benefit. Through this program, schools enter into voluntary agreements with VA to pay a portion of the tuition and fees that exceed an individual's Post-9/11 GI Bill benefit and VA matches the school's contribution. 38 U.S.C. § 3317.

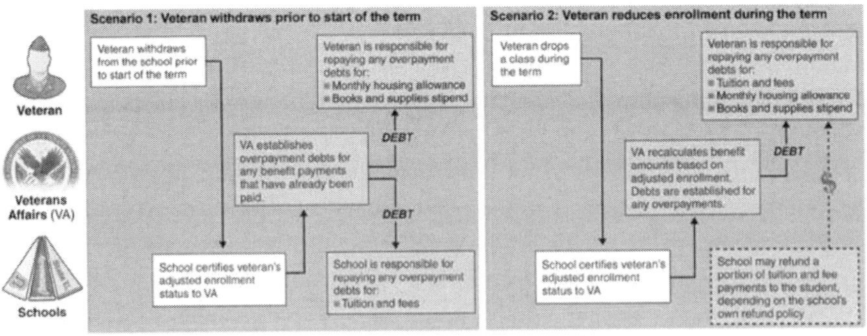

Source: GAO analysis of VA Documents. GAO (images). | GAO-16-42.

Figure 2. Examples of Post-9/11 GI Bill Overpayment Scenarios.

When an overpayment is caused by an enrollment change, VA establishes an overpayment debt for the veteran, the school, or both depending on the circumstances (see fig. 2).

VA Collection Process

Overpayment debts are forwarded to VA's centralized collection office, the Debt Management Center, for collection. Once schools or veterans receive a collection letter from the Debt Management Center, they can arrange to repay the debt in full, set up a payment plan, dispute the existence or amount of the debt, or request a waiver of the debt due to financial hardship or special circumstances.[15] If schools or veterans do not initiate one of these options to address the debt, VA begins pursuing more aggressive collection methods. These can include offsetting—that is, reducing or withholding—future Post-9/11 GI Bill payments or tax returns and reporting debts to credit rating agencies, as illustrated in figure 3. Since veterans are liable for most overpayments, VA collects debts from hundreds of thousands of individual veterans.

Comparison with Department of Education Processes

We have previously compared VA's processes to those of the Department of Education.[16] The Department of Education uses a different structure than VA for processing and collecting federal student aid overpayments. In contrast to VA, Education generally works directly with schools to return overpayments of federal student aid funds, focusing its collection efforts on a few thousand schools rather than working directly with hundreds of thousands of students. The Department of Education payment systems also allow schools to reconcile any enrollment changes before the term by adjusting the school's aggregate receipt of federal student aid funds, rather than issuing individual debts and new payments to the school. In contrast, VA processes each tuition payment and collection separately.

In reaction to our prior work comparing VA's processes with the Department of Education's, VA officials raised concerns about adopting similar practices to the Department of Education.

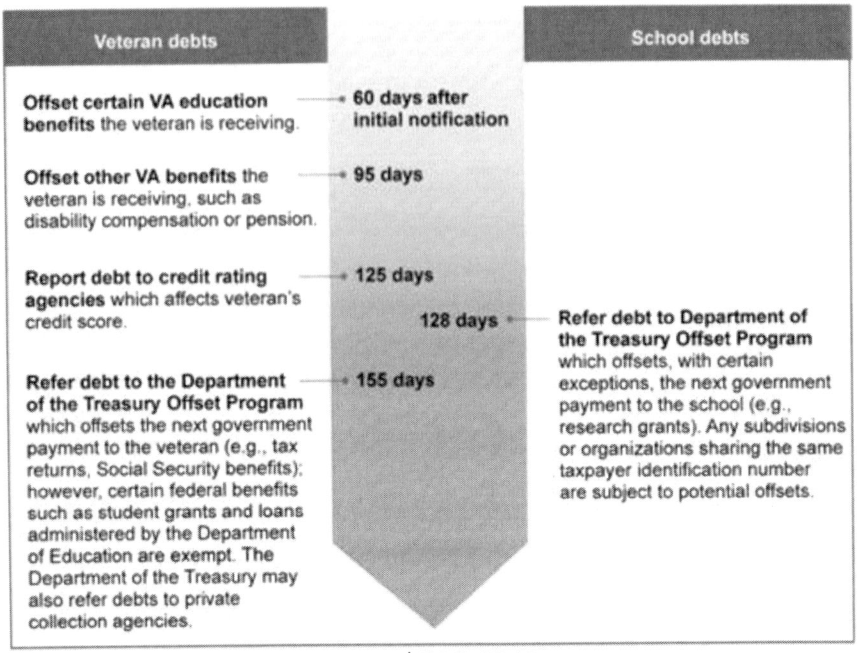

Source: GAO analysisof VA documents. | GAO-15-42.

Notes: This timeline can vary based on how long it takes for debts to be transferred from the regional processing offices to the Debt Management Center for collection. For this figure we included 5 days for the transfer process, which VA officials said can take between 2 to10 days.

Post-9/11 GI Bill tuition and fee payments to schools are exempt from offsets. Offsets to VA compensation and pension benefits do not follow a standard timeline, since they are identified through a monthly data match, but would not begin until 95 days after a veteran's initial notification.

Figure 3. Timeline for VA Collection Actions When Overpayment Debts Are Not Otherwise Repaid.

For example, according to VA officials if VA started collecting all tuition overpayments from schools, schools would still be able to bill veterans for overpayment debts and potentially would not allow veterans to reenroll for class until these debts were repaid. In addition, veterans would have to repay any overpayment debts to their school out-of-pocket, rather than through offsets to their Post-9/11 GI Bill housing payments.

VA IDENTIFIED OVER $400 MILLION IN POST-9/11 GI BILL OVERPAYMENTS IN FISCAL YEAR 2014 AND DOES NOT EFFECTIVELY MONITOR THESE DEBTS

One in Four Beneficiaries and 6,000 Schools Incurred Overpayments in Fiscal Year 2014, Caused Primarily by Veteran Enrollment Changes after VA's Initial Payments

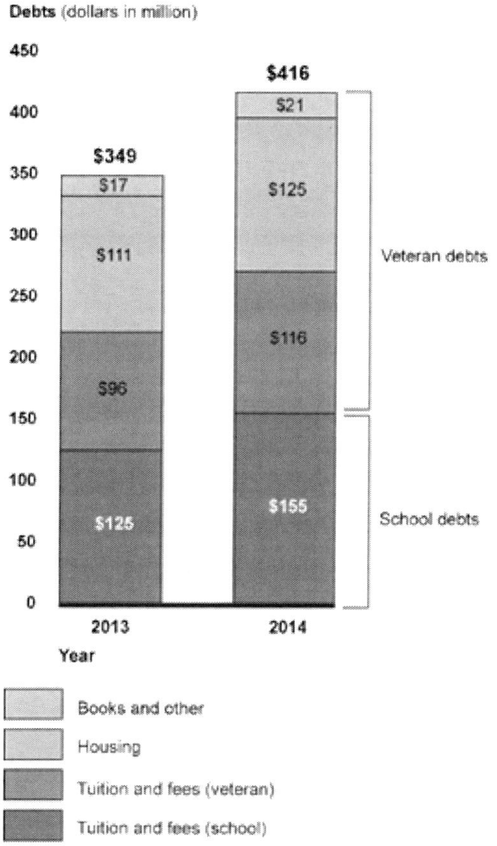

Source: GAO analysis of VA payment data. | GAO-16-42.

Note: Individual amounts for 2014 do not sum to $416 million due to rounding. The "other" benefits category includes fees for student licensing or certification tests and national tests (e.g., SAT, GRE, LSAT).

Figure 4. Amount and Type of Post-9/11 GI Bill Overpayments to Veterans and Schools, Fiscal Years 2013 and 2014.

VA made $416 million in Post-9/11 GI Bill overpayments in fiscal year 2014, or 4 percent of the over $10 billion in benefits paid during that period. The bulk of these overpayments went to veterans instead of schools, as shown in figure 4.[17] Overpayments increased by nearly 20 percent from fiscal year 2013 to 2014, the only 2 years for which data were available, while total program payments increased by just 6 percent.

Most overpayments are caused by veteran enrollment changes, over which VA has limited control. In these cases, VA's original payments were correct based on the veteran's planned enrollment, but some or all of the original payment became an overpayment when the veteran subsequently dropped a class or withdrew from school. VA estimated that veteran enrollment changes caused 90 percent of high-dollar Post-9/11 GI Bill overpayments (see fig. 5).[18] The remaining high-dollar overpayments were caused by school reporting errors (e.g., submitting incorrect enrollment or tuition information) and VA processing errors (e.g., duplicate payments or data entry errors).[19]

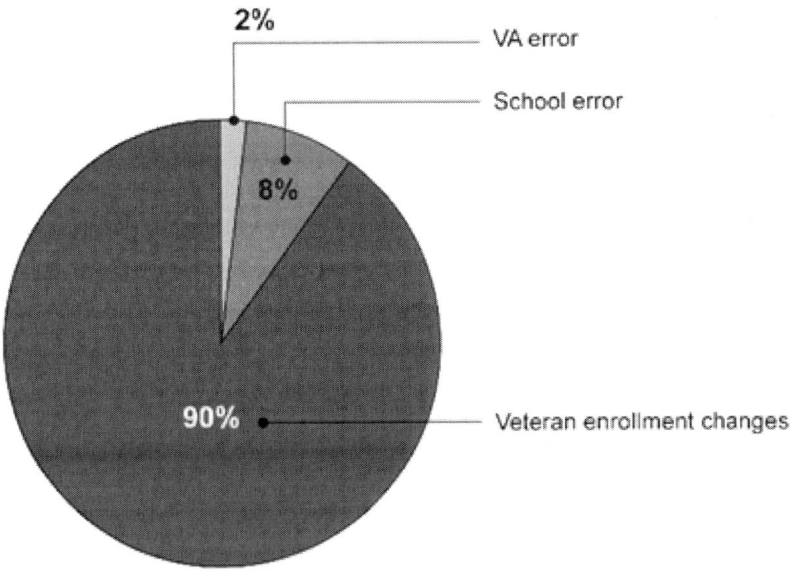

Source: GAO analysis of Vas Qarterly High-Dollar Overpayment Reports. | GAO-16-42.

Note: VA's estimates are based on a sample with a 95 percent confidence level and a ± 5 percent confidence interval.

Figure 5. Causes of Post-9/11 GI Bill High-Dollar Overpayments, Fiscal Years 2013 and 2014.

Approximately 1 out of 4 beneficiaries incurred an overpayment in fiscal year 2014—more than 225,000 veterans. The median amount that veterans had to repay was about $570, which could correspond to dropping a single class during the term and can be a sizable debt for a college student with limited income. Some veterans incurred much larger overpayments. For example, over 7,000 veterans had overpayments of more than $5,000, which can occur when a veteran completely withdraws from school or receives several months of housing overpayments (see fig. 6).

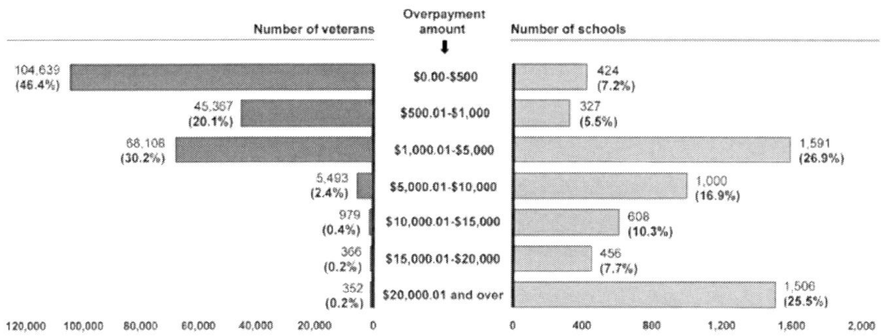

Source: GAO analysis of VA payment data. | GAO-16-42.

Figure 6. Distribution of Post-9/11 GI Bill Overpayment Debt Amounts, Fiscal Year 2014.

Almost 6,000 schools incurred overpayments in fiscal year 2014, often for multiple veterans, with a total median debt of $7,800 per school. School overpayments arise when veterans never attended classes or withdrew from school on or before the start date, although they can also be caused by VA and school error in certain cases. About 5 percent of schools accounted for almost half of all school overpayments.[20]

VA Has $152 Million in Uncollected Overpayment Debt from Fiscal Year 2014 and an Additional $110 Million from Prior Years, Primarily Owed by Veterans

VA had $262 million in outstanding Post-9/11 GI Bill overpayment debts, as of November 2014, primarily owed by veterans. More than half of these uncollected debts are from overpayments that occurred in fiscal year 2014, some of which were still in the initial stages of collection and likely have been repaid since VA provided these data. VA has had more time to collect debts from prior years. However, $110 million in uncollected debts are older than 1 year, some of which date back to 2010 (see fig. 7).

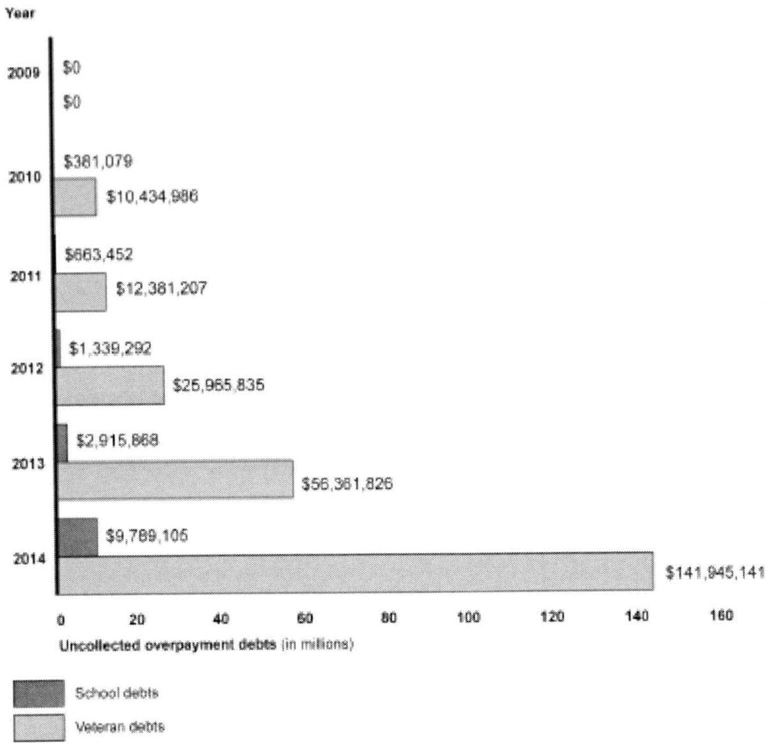

Source: GAO analysis of VA payment and collection data. | GAO-16-42.

Figure 7. Uncollected Post-9/11 GI Bill Overpayment Debts by Year of Origin, as of November 2014.

Veterans are responsible for the vast majority of uncollected overpayment debts since VA has less success collecting debts from veterans than from schools. Of the total amount outstanding, more than 90 percent was owed by veterans rather than owed by schools. Schools had already repaid almost all of the overpayment debts they incurred in fiscal years 2013 and 2014, while veterans had so far repaid 75 percent of overpayments from fiscal year 2013 and 46 percent from 2014.[21] School overpayments are generally collected through direct payments (e.g., check, credit card, electronic funds transfer), while veteran overpayments are collected through several methods, most commonly by deducting the debt amounts from subsequent GI Bill or other VA payments. VA also collected from veterans through direct payments, offsetting other federal payments such as federal tax returns, and private debt collection agencies.[22]

VA Does Not Monitor the Full Extent of Overpayments and Collections, Which Hinders Its Ability to Manage the Post-9/11 GI Bill Program

VA does not monitor the full extent of Post-9/11 GI Bill overpayments and collections. For example, VA does not regularly track the number of overpayments or the amount of uncollected student debts.[23] Although VA was able to provide this information in response to our data request, it is not something the agency actively monitors on a regular basis. VA has instead focused its current monitoring efforts on one subset of overpayments, those that are considered "improper." As it is legally required to do, VA reports an estimated improper payment rate for different benefit programs.[24] While these rates are a useful government-wide accountability measure, they do not capture the vast majority of Post-9/11 GI Bill overpayments that occur due to subsequent enrollment changes.[25] The approximately 90 percent of overpayments resulting from veteran enrollment changes are not categorized as improper since the payments are correct when issued and only become overpayments at a later date after the veteran makes an enrollment change. As a result, VA's estimated improper payment rate for the Post-9/11 GI Bill provides little insight into the over $400 million in overpayments the agency made in fiscal year 2014. As for collections, the only specific data on the Post-9/11 GI Bill that the Debt Management Center actively monitors is for school debts, which only account for about a third of program overpayments.[26] VA officials do not regularly monitor collection rates for student overpayments, which represent the majority of uncollected debts.

VA's limited monitoring of overpayments and collections makes it difficult to effectively manage the Post-9/11 GI Bill program. OMB Circular A-129 instructs all federal agencies to use comprehensive reports on the status of overpayments and other receivables to monitor their effectiveness and enable data-driven decision making.[27] VA's limited monitoring efforts fall short of this standard. VA's ability to monitor historical trends in overpayments and collections is in some ways constrained by the limitations of its data systems. Specifically, debts are removed from VA's main payment and collection database and archived 2 years after repayment. While this limits the availability of summary information for analyzing prior historical trends and performance, VA could replicate the analysis we conducted for this study by periodically calculating key measures from the available data records. One area where VA has made some strides is by monitoring school debts on a monthly basis. However, as evidenced by its significantly limited monitoring activity, VA has not prioritized the need to actively monitor veteran overpayments and collections for the Post 9/11 GI Bill program, although VA officials acknowledged that additional monitoring would help improve program management. By not actively monitoring available data on overpayments and collections, VA cannot assess its efforts to reduce overpayments nor can it gauge the effectiveness of its collection efforts. This also limits VA's ability to proactively manage the program to address overpayment or collection issues, for example, by identifying trends and targeting outreach to the small number of schools that account for the majority of overpayment dollars.

Inadequate Guidance, Controls, and Training Have Limited VA's Effectiveness in Reducing Overpayments from Enrollment Changes and School Errors

VA Lacks Adequate Guidance and Controls That Could Reduce Overpayments from Enrollment Changes

Despite enrollment changes being responsible for most overpayments, VA provides limited guidance to veterans about the possible consequences of enrollment changes. Staff from VA's Debt Management Center and its Education Call Center, as well as staff who conduct school compliance surveys, said that many veterans who incur overpayments as a result of enrollment changes may not realize that they are doing so. VA informs veterans about their potential liability for overpayment debts resulting from enrollment changes in the letter it sends veterans when they become eligible for benefits. VA also posts responses to some overpayment-related questions on the Post-9/11 GI Bill website.

However, VA does not explain—either in the benefits letter, on the Post-9/11 GI Bill website, or in other places veterans are likely to seek program information—how to avoid creating debts once enrolled in school. The letter veterans receive simply tells them that they are responsible for all debts resulting from reductions or terminations of their enrollment. It does not explain, for example, the difference between VA overpayments and school refund policies or that failure to promptly notify VA of enrollment changes can increase the incidence and amount of housing overpayments. In addition, VA does not disclose its formula for calculating overpayments in any of the guidance it provides to veterans or schools, which makes it difficult for veterans—and school certifying officials who advise them—to accurately estimate the potential tuition overpayments veterans might incur for dropping a class. In contrast, VA requires schools to include information about school refund policies for unused tuition and fee payments in information available to all veterans.[28]

As a result, officials at two of the schools we interviewed said that the majority of overpayment issues arise among new student veterans who are not aware of the consequences of enrollment changes until after they have already incurred their first overpayment debt. In other cases, veterans are confused about when overpayments are created. For example, staff from VA's Debt Management Center explained that some veterans incorrectly think they will not incur a debt if they drop a class before their school's deadline to add or drop classes.[29] Moreover, our review of complaints veterans have made to VA also demonstrates some veterans' confusion about how the Post-9/11 GI Bill works.[30] For example, one veteran was shocked to learn he had incurred a debt of over $5,000 stemming from his enrollment changes. According to federal internal control standards, all agencies should ensure they are using adequate means of communicating with external stakeholders who may have a significant impact on the agency achieving its goals.[31] If VA does not enhance its guidance to veterans about its overpayments policies, veterans may continue to incur debts that could be avoided.

VA has an optional process for schools to report veteran enrollments that can help prevent overpayments due to enrollment changes, but only a small proportion of schools currently use it. Typically, a school certifying official sends a veteran's enrollment information (e.g., tuition, fees, term dates) to VA soon after a veteran enrolls in an upcoming term. Once VA processes the claim and makes tuition and fee payments to the school, any subsequent enrollment changes can create overpayments. As an alternative, VA gives schools the option of using a two-stage process, called dual-certification. Schools can initially precertify a veteran's enrollment for $0 for tuition and fees before the term begins, which allows VA to start paying housing benefits without delay.

The school can then recertify the enrollment with the actual tuition and fees amount at a later date—e.g., after the period to add or drop classes ends when many enrollment changes have already occurred. Since VA does not send tuition payments until the school certifies an actual tuition and fee amount, dual-certification can help prevent tuition overpayments that occur when a veteran drops a class at the beginning of the term.

Despite the potential benefits, dual-certification has not been widely adopted, in part because VA's guidance to schools does not explain the benefits of using this process. According to a 2013 survey by the National Association of College and University Business Officers, 30 percent of the 239 schools responding to the survey reported that they used dualcertification.[32] Only one of the nine schools we interviewed uses this approach, and an official at this school said that switching to the dual-certification process was responsible for reducing the school's overpayment amount from $500,000 to $50,000 each semester. In contrast, six of the schools we interviewed send tuition and fee information to VA by the start of the term.[33] An official at one of these schools does not like to use dual-certification because it requires submitting enrollment information to VA twice. A VA official further explained that many schools want to be paid up front, so they submit the course enrollment and expected tuition and fees before the term. Recognizing that dual-certification may not work well for some schools, given the additional work involved and delay in receiving tuition payments, VA does not require this approach. Nevertheless, this can be a useful option for some schools and VA's guidance to schools does not explain how dual certification can prevent overpayments. Internal control standards stipulate that adequate communication with external parties through guidance and other methods is essential for achieving agency goals.[34] By not providing guidance to schools about the benefits of using dual-certification, VA is missing an opportunity to reduce a potentially large number of overpayments as well as the burden placed on veterans and schools to repay those debts.

Finally, unlike most other GI Bill programs, VA has not required veterans in traditional degree and certificate programs using the Post-9/11 GI Bill to regularly verify their enrollment throughout the school term, which exacerbates the incidence and amount of housing benefit overpayments due to delayed reporting of enrollment changes.[35] When veterans reduce their enrollment, they continue to receive housing benefit overpayments each month until VA is notified of the change.[36] Even though VA's guidance to veterans instructs them to promptly notify their school certifying official and VA of any enrollment changes, they do not always do so. In one case file we reviewed, the veteran withdrew from school one day before the term began in mid-August, but the enrollment change was not reported to VA until late October. As a result, this veteran received an extra 2 months of housing benefits after withdrawing, which created an overpayment of over $3,000. In another case file review, a veteran's enrollment changes were reported to VA 3 months after they happened. As a result the veteran incurred a housing overpayment of $2,200. These housing overpayments would have been avoided if veterans using the Post-9/11 GI Bill were required to verify their monthly enrollment.

VA officials said they would like to require veterans using the Post-9/11 GI Bill to verify their monthly enrollment but would need to develop a new verification process.[37] One option VA has considered is developing a new online system, but VA officials said the agency has not yet developed the system due to budgetary constraints. A VA contractor estimated in 2013 that it would cost approximately $10 million to implement an online verification system, although VA officials were unsure if this estimate is still accurate. Such an investment would provide substantial long-term savings for VA in comparison with the current system by reducing housing overpayments and also help VA comply with federal requirements to establish practices that ensure funds are safeguarded against waste or loss.[38] For example, VA made almost $111 million in housing overpayments in fiscal year 2013, almost $29 million of which was still uncollected as of November 2014. Although requiring veterans to verify their enrollment would not eliminate all of these overpayments, if the contractor's prior cost estimates are still correct, the new system could still pay for itself in 1 year if it reduced uncollected housing overpayments by just one-third. The potential savings from an enrollment verification system would likely increase in future years as the size of the Post-9/11 GI Bill program continues to grow, creating a long term benefit for VA and taxpayers. Federal internal control standards state that agencies need effective policies and procedures to help achieve results and ensure stewardship of government resources.[39]

School Officials with Inadequate Training Contribute to Reporting Errors

Schools cause overpayments when they make processing errors, such as reporting the wrong enrollment dates or billing VA for non-allowable fees. VA estimated that these errors account for 8 percent of high-dollar overpayment cases in fiscal years 2013 and 2014, while we estimated that they account for around $28 million of the $280 million in high-dollar overpayments VA made in fiscal year 2014.[40] School errors also accounted for over half of the overpayment findings in VA's initial analysis of compliance surveys conducted in fiscal years 2014 and 2015. Similarly, we identified a variety of school errors that resulted in overpayments among the 24 compliance surveys we reviewed. For example, in one compliance survey, the school certifying official did not know how to correctly report the last day of the school term, resulting in overpayments of $7,000, $4,000, and $3,500 for three different students. School officials can also create overpayments when they are unfamiliar with what types of school fees VA allows under the Post-9/11 GI Bill program. For example, in one school compliance survey we reviewed, a school certifying official billed VA $200 for non-allowable book fees for multiple students. At another school, the school certifying official billed VA for a variety of unallowable fees, all of which resulted in overpayments. VA compliance survey specialists used these reviews to educate school officials on VA payment policies and sometimes recommended that the school certifying officials obtain additional training.

School officials without adequate training were commonly cited as a source of school errors in our interviews with staff from VA's Regional Processing Office and Debt Management Center. Regional processing office staff described some common errors made by school certifying officials. For example, some school officials do not adjust the tuition or fee amount when reporting an enrollment change; they submit conflicting information in the comments field; and they sometimes report the wrong withdrawal date (e.g., using the date the form was submitted, rather than when the enrollment change occurred). VA Debt Management Center staff stated that school certifying officials often have trouble reporting enrollment changes correctly and could benefit from additional training on Post-9/11 GI Bill policies. For example, school certifying officials sometimes do not understand that veterans will incur an overpayment for dropping classes after the term has begun and are often confused by VA's definition of school terms. Compliance survey officials noted that there is a high level of turnover among school certifying officials, and that staff who are new to the job face a steep learning curve. Additionally, a 2014 VA Inspector General report identified multiple school reporting errors and noted that if school certifying officials completed VA's recommended training, it could improve the timeliness and accuracy of their submitted claims.[41]

VA offers a variety of training opportunities for school officials, but VA officials said the agency lacks the authority to require that school certifying officials complete any of its training about how to correctly process enrollment information, despite the fact that the Post-9/11 GI Bill program is complex for schools to administer and that schools caused an estimated $28 million in high-dollar overpayments in fiscal year 2014. In addition to publishing a handbook for school certifying officials, VA offers a 40-hour, self-paced, online course to provide a comprehensive overview of schools' responsibilities and GI Bill payment processes.[42] Prior GAO and VA Inspector General reports have recommended that VA do more to encourage school certifying officials to take advantage of VA training opportunities. While VA has taken some steps to address these recommendations and officials said they have conducted outreach through conferences and workshops, the number of school officials completing VA's online training remains low.[43] In 2014, only 29 percent of school certifying officials (666 of 2,259) who accessed this training completed it; the same percentage have completed the training so far in 2015 (358 of 1,218 as of June 2015). According to VA officials, VA lacks direct legal authority to require school certifying officials to complete a minimum level of training on how to implement the program, although they indicated that they would like the ability to do so. However, school officials have essential duties in processing Post-9/11 GI Bill payments and need to possess and maintain a level of competence to do their job, which includes receiving training. This would be consistent with federal internal control standards.[44] In the absence of minimum level training requirements for school officials, VA lacks reasonable assurance that staff with key responsibilities in the payment process know how to avoid creating overpayments.

VA Uses Quality Controls to Address Internal Processing Errors

VA causes overpayments when it issues a duplicate payment or makes data entry errors regarding tuition or fee amounts, training time, and other key enrollment data. VA estimated that these errors caused 2 percent of the high-dollar overpayment cases in fiscal years 2013 and 2014 and we estimated that they account for around $6 million of the $280 million in high-dollar overpayments VA made in fiscal year 2014.[45] In one of the case files we reviewed, a veteran had to repay $7,200 in tuition debt because VA erroneously calculated a larger benefit than he was eligible for based on his years of service. In another case, VA sent a tuition payment to the wrong school, which the school then had to repay. In the case of a veteran housing overpayment we reviewed, VA accidentally processed a veteran's enrollment certification twice, so that it looked like he was enrolled for more classes than he actually was. As a result of this error, VA provided housing payments to the veteran, although he should have been ineligible because he was enrolled less than half-time.[46] The veteran ended up with a $3,000 overpayment when the error was detected.

VA has taken steps to address processing errors through technology improvements, quality assurance reviews, and training. For example, agency investments in technology improvements have allowed a proportion of claims to be processed automatically, reducing the possibility of human error, according to VA officials. In fiscal year 2014, VA automatically processed 51 percent of Post-9/11 GI Bill claims. VA also monitors overall payment accuracy at the four regional offices. A quality assurance team reviews a sample of 25 Post-9/11 GI Bill payments from each regional office every quarter. VA officials said any common errors identified during these reviews are addressed through additional training or guidance. In addition, officials from the regional office we visited said that each month they review five claims processed by each employee to monitor payment accuracy. VA also ensures that claims processers stay up-to-date on program policies by requiring 24 hours of refresher training each year.

A'S NOTIFICATION METHODS AND OVERPAYMENT CALCULATIONS HAMPER ITS COLLECTION EFFORTS

VA's Notification Methods Can Leave Veterans and Schools Unaware of Their Overpayment Debts

VA relies on mailed letters to notify veterans and schools of overpayments, which can leave some veterans and schools unaware of their debts until VA begins collecting them. Once an overpayment debt is created, VA mails a sequence of letters to notify the responsible veteran or school of their debt. For veterans, these letters are generally sent to the addresses listed on their initial application for Post-9/11 GI Bill benefits, according to VA officials.[47] However, students are a highly transient population and Post-9/11 GI Bill benefits can be used over multiple years, so for many veterans the addresses VA relies on may no longer be accurate, according to VA and school officials.

When veterans do not receive notification letters for their debts, they may not know they have a debt, causing them to miss key deadlines. Specifically, VA will not suspend collection actions if a veteran requests a waiver or disputes the amount of a debt more than 30 days after the initial notification letter. Then, if VA begins collecting the debt by offsetting other benefits, such as monthly housing payments, veterans may be unprepared and unable to cover their expenses, potentially creating financial obstacles towards continuing their education, according to officials from veteran service organizations. Although VA does not keep data on undeliverable mail, VA call center staff said they frequently receive calls from veterans who were unaware of their overpayment debts until their federal tax returns were offset, which makes it difficult for these veterans to proactively plan and budget for how to cover their living expenses in light of impending collections. If veterans do not receive a notification letter, these deadlines will pass without the veterans' knowledge, leaving them with limited recourse to halt collection actions and potentially having negative effects on their credit rating.[48]

For schools, VA mails the letters to the school's central address, leaving the school responsible for directing the letter to the appropriate administrator or office. However, some school administrators told us that these letters sometimes get lost in transit, putting schools at risk of having future federal grants offset for collection. These problems with mailed letters not only create complications for veterans and schools, but they also make it more difficult for VA to collect debts since veterans and schools are less likely to repay their debts in a timely manner if they are unaware that the debts exist.

VA is required to notify veterans and schools of any debts in writing.[49] According to federal internal control standards, all agencies should ensure they are using adequate means of communicating with external stakeholders.[50] To effectively communicate with veterans and schools, VA may also need to use other notification methods in addition to mailed letters. For example, administrators at six of the nine schools we interviewed expressed a preference for VA to use electronic rather than mailed correspondence.[51] Students are also generally accustomed to electronic communication, as one school official noted, and could benefit from electronic communication, therefore alleviating potential issues with out-of-date mailing addresses. VA already has existing online portals that could be leveraged to inform veterans and schools about their overpayment debts. VA's eBenefits portal, for example, already provides over 3 million veterans with access to personalized information about their VA benefits. VA officials said this system could be upgraded to provide veterans with online access to debt notification letters; however, the agency has not implemented this proposal due to other funding priorities.[52] Officials at six of the nine schools we interviewed suggested email as another potential low cost option; however, VA would need a mechanism to ensure it is using up-to-date email addresses. By not pursuing alternative mechanisms to supplement mailed letters, significant numbers of veterans and schools may remain unaware of their overpayment debts and unprepared for the financial consequences, which could also complicate and prolong VA's collection efforts.

VA's debt notification letters also provide essential information in two separate letters, making it difficult for veterans and schools to reconcile and repay overpayment debts. VA is required to provide debtors with information on the amount of the debt, the reason for the debt, their right to dispute the debt or request a waiver, and how to repay it.[53] However, VA conveys this information in two separate letters, neither of which contains all the information a veteran or school needs to understand the overpayment and how to repay it (see fig. 8). For example, VA's regional offices mail veterans an initial notification letter which includes information on the amount and cause of their overpayment debt. However, it is not until more than 30 days later that VA's debt collection office mails the veteran a second letter with information on how to repay the debt, according to VA officials. Since each of these letters only provides veterans with half of the information they need, they can create confusion. Specifically, VA debt collection staff said they frequently receive questions from veterans who are confused because information on the cause of overpayments and the collection process is conveyed in separate letters. For example, officials from the debt collection call center said one of the most common questions they receive from veterans is to ask why their debt was established, since this information is not included in the second letter veterans receive from the debt collection office. This delay in receiving all of the information associated with their debt could also delay the collection process since veterans may be less likely to repay their debts until they understand both the cause of overpayments and have the information they need on how to repay them. VA similarly mails this information to schools in two separate letters, and school officials told us this creates some confusion since they must wait to repay any overpayment debts until they can match up both letters from VA, which can also delay collections. One school administrator told us that it can be particularly difficult to keep track of the two separate letters at larger schools that enroll thousands of veterans, so they had to hire two new staff to deal with the administrative burden of researching overpayment debts.

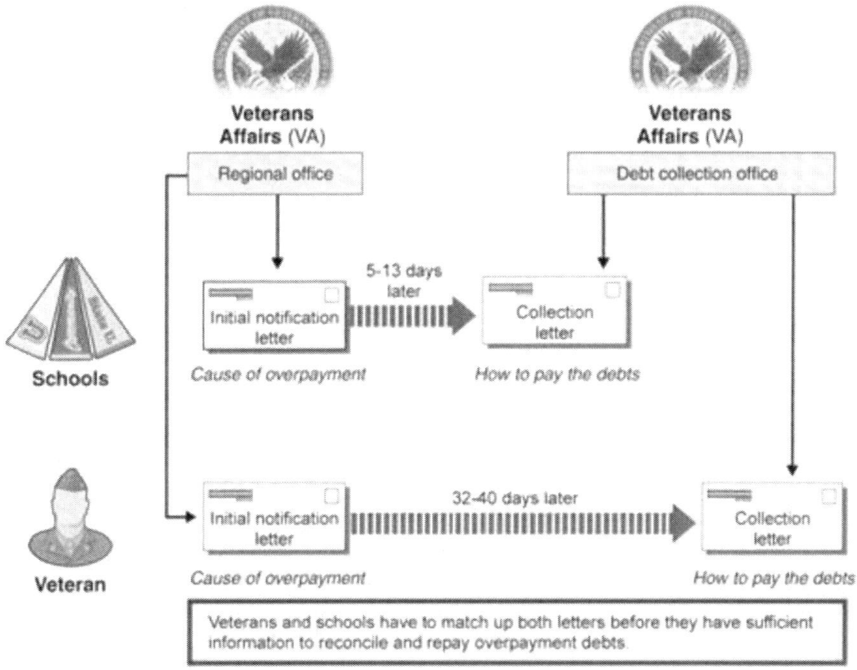

Source: GAO analysis of VA guidance and agency interviews. (GAO) (images).
| AO-16-42.

Figure 8. Process for Notifying Veterans and Schools of Overpayment Debts.

VA officials said the initial notification letters are sent separately from the debt collection letters to promptly notify veterans about their debts and to allow veterans time to dispute them. Although this may justify sending two separate letters, it would still help avoid confusion for veterans and schools if the later debt collection letters included information on both the cause of the overpayment and repayment options. The collection letters mailed by VA's debt collection office do not include details on the cause of debts because VA's regional offices do not currently share this information when referring debts for collection. Officials from VA's debt collection office told us they would like to include some basic information on the cause of debts in their letters, such as the term dates associated with a veteran withdrawal. However, VA officials responsible for administering the Post-9/11 GI Bill said the cause of the overpayments is already clearly communicated in the initial notification letters. Nevertheless, this should not preclude the regional processing offices from sharing basic information on the causes of overpayments so it could be included in subsequent letters along with information on how to repay debts. Given VA's regulatory requirement to provide students and schools with information on both the cause of their debts and how to repay them, VA could improve its efforts to convey this information. This would also be consistent with federal internal control standards for information sharing. The current lack of information sharing between offices limits VA's ability to communicate both the overpayment cause and repayment options in at least one of the letters VA sends to veterans and schools. This process can lead to confusion and cause delays in veterans and schools repaying their debts in a timely manner.

VA's Formula for Prorating Tuition Overpayments Reduces Total Collections

VA's formula for prorating overpayments gives veterans credit for extra days of attendance after they drop a class, thereby reducing the amount subject to collection. When a Post-9/11 GI Bill beneficiary drops a class during the term, VA prorates the resulting overpayment as though the veteran attended class through the end of the month rather than using the actual date of the withdrawal.[54] For example, if a student drops a class on September 1, VA would prorate the overpayment amount as though the student had been enrolled through September 30. This in effect credits students for up to 30 extra days of classes they did not attend, which can reduce the overpayment amount subject to collection by hundreds of dollars per veteran (see fig. 9). VA officials said this policy was designed for monthly housing benefits, and then applied to tuition benefits that are paid separately under the Post-9/11 GI Bill. Although crediting a student for a full month of enrollment may be appropriate for benefits that are paid on a monthly basis, such as housing, it is less appropriate for benefits that are paid as up-front lump sums, such as tuition, particularly since the law stipulates that education benefits shall only be paid for the period of time during which the veteran is enrolled.[55] Since VA's overpayment calculation is crediting veterans for school days they did not attend, it is inappropriately increasing the cost of the program.

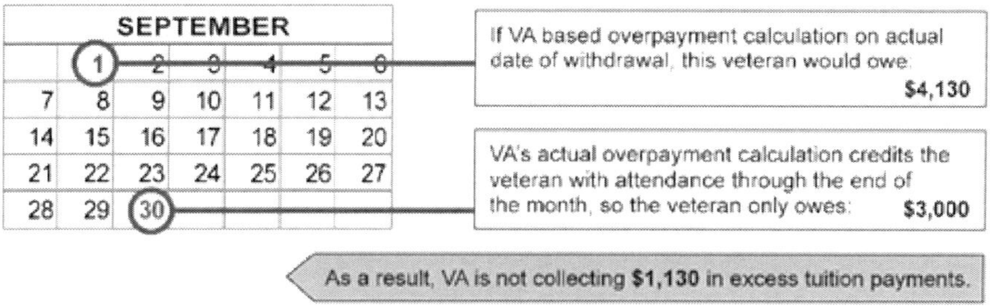

Source: GAO analysis of VA guidance. | GAO-16-42.

Figure 9. Effect of Prorating Overpayments Based on the End of the Month.

In addition, VA's formula for prorating overpayment amounts does not account for schools' own internal refund policies, and can sometimes result in veterans receiving surplus funds that VA is not collecting. Some schools have fairly generous tuition refund policies when students drop a class or withdraw from school early in the term. In these cases, a school may send the veteran a tuition refund that is larger than the overpayment amount the veteran owes to VA, leaving the veteran with a potential financial gain. For example, one of the community colleges we examined provided a 100 percent tuition refund if a student withdrew within the first two and a half weeks of the term, so a veteran withdrawing from school would receive a full refund of $2,100 from the school. However, VA will create an overpayment debt of $1,750 for this veteran since they had attended two and half weeks of the 15 week term before withdrawing.[56]

This would leave the veteran in this example with an extra $350 after repaying their overpayment debt. The excess tuition payments VA is not collecting are even larger at schools with higher tuition rates (see fig. 10).

Three of the nine schools included in our review had institutional refund policies that provided all students with a 100 percent refund for withdrawals within the first two or three weeks of the term.[57] Officials at one of these schools estimated that the difference between their refund policy and VA's overpayment calculations had resulted in over $136,000 in excess tuition payments for 53 veterans between 2009 and 2014, averaging over $2,500 per veteran. These officials said they had attempted to return these excess funds to VA, but VA would not accept them. Officials at another school said they attempt to return any excess funds to VA three times, but since VA usually will not accept these funds, the school eventually just gives them to the veteran. VA officials told us they cannot accept funds in excess of the overpayment debt that is billed to veterans and said that some of these situations might occur when schools do not correctly account for school refund policies when reporting enrollment and tuition changes. The Post-9/11 GI Bill's authorizing statute specifies that benefits are only payable in an amount equal to the actual cost of tuition and fees charged by the institution, but in these cases VA's tuition and fees payments exceed the amounts charged by the schools once the refund policies are accounted for—that is, VA is making payments for tuition amounts that were not charged by the school.[58] As a result, VA is overpaying for tuition and these excess funds are being retained by schools or returned to veterans rather than collected by VA.

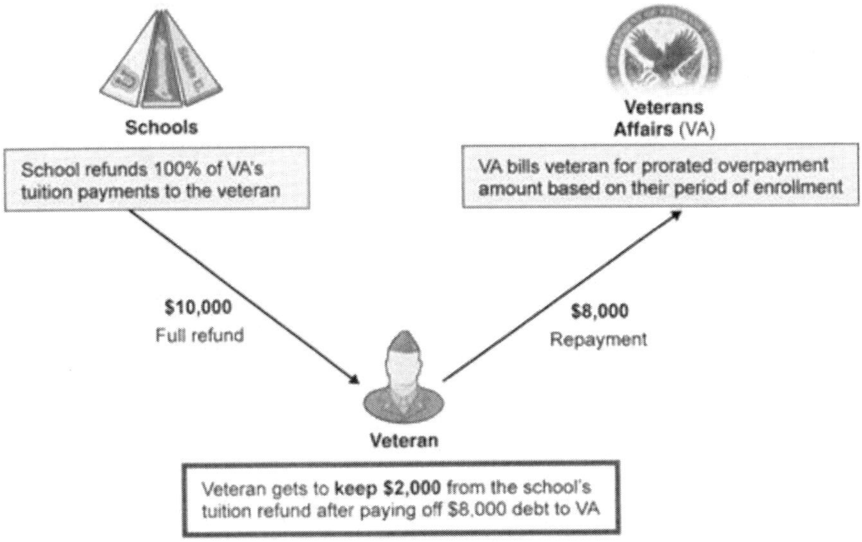

Source: GAO analysis of VA guidance. GAO (images). | GAO-16-42.

Figure 10. Overpayment Example when Veteran Withdraws during School's 100 Percent Refund Period.

Conclusion

The Post-9/11 GI Bill has provided valuable education benefits to millions of veterans, but the program's structure of collecting debts directly from veterans creates certain risks. Although the program could have been designed differently from the beginning to avoid some of the subsequent problems with overpayments, at this point, a complete overhaul, such as collecting tuition and fee overpayments directly from schools, would require significant restructuring of VA's payment operations as well as legislative changes. However, current problems with overpayments can still be addressed through process improvements and proactive management on the part of VA. For example, VA currently collects and monitors only limited data on Post-9/11 GI Bill overpayments and collections, overlooking the most common types of overpayments and collections. Overpayments increased to over $400 million in fiscal year 2014, affecting approximately one in four beneficiaries. Effective program management requires monitoring of key data elements. Unless VA expands its monitoring of overpayment debts and collections, it will not be able to ensure that it is taking appropriate steps to safeguard taxpayer funds.

Overpayments are an inevitable byproduct of the Post-9/11 GI Bill since some veteran enrollment changes are to be expected. However, there are ways that VA can reduce the number and amount of future overpayments.

For example, if VA provided more information to veterans about potential overpayment debts, veterans would better understand the financial consequences of dropping a class or withdrawing from school and could take steps to avoid some overpayments. In addition, VA provides schools with an optional process for certifying tuition and fees that could reduce the effect of enrollment changes, although it does not explain in its guidance to schools the potential advantages of this process. Moreover, since veterans using the Post-9/11 GI Bill are not required to regularly verify their enrollment, overpayments from enrollment changes are also magnified by any delays in reporting these changes to VA since veterans continue to receive monthly housing payments. These potentially avoidable overpayments will continue to occur unless VA proactively addresses issues associated with enrollment changes. Similarly, unnecessary school reporting errors will lead to overpayments if school certifying officials do not receive appropriate training to understand VA's payment and reporting processes. Although VA offers online training that would address these issues, school officials are not required to take part in this minimum level of training, because VA officials believe the agency does not have the statutory authority to require them to do so.

VA is responsible for recovering all debts in an efficient and effective manner, but these efforts are hampered by the processes VA uses to notify and collect debts from veterans and schools. Mailed letters alone are not an effective method of notifying students and schools, particularly since other electronic options are also available. This can leave veterans unaware of their debts and create financial hardships for them when VA offsets other income sources to collect these debts. In addition, the lack of a single source of information on both the cause of debts and repayment options creates unnecessary confusion for veterans that can lead to delays in repayment as well as an administrative burden for schools. Finally, VA also needs to ensure that it is appropriately calculating overpayment debts in accordance with the law and recovers any excess payments. However, VA's current method of calculating overpayments credits veterans for extra days of attendance and does not account for school refund policies, which unnecessarily increases the cost of the program.

MATTER FOR CONGRESSIONAL CONSIDERATION

To address Post-9/11 GI Bill overpayments resulting from school errors, Congress should consider granting VA explicit authority to require a minimum level of training for appropriate school officials.

RECOMMENDATIONS FOR EXECUTIVE ACTION

To improve the administration of the Post-9/11 GI Bill, reduce the occurrence of overpayments, and increase debt collections, we recommend that the Secretary of Veterans Affairs take the following eight actions:

Improve program management by:

- Expanding monitoring of available information on overpayment debts and collections. This could include regularly tracking the number and amount of overpayments created and the effectiveness of collection efforts.

Address overpayments resulting from enrollment changes by:

- Providing guidance to educate student veterans about their benefits and consequences of changing their enrollment.
- Providing guidance to schools about the benefits of using a dual certification process where schools wait to certify the actual tuition and fee amounts until after the school's deadline for adding and dropping classes.

- Identifying and implementing a cost-effective way to allow Post-9/11 GI Bill beneficiaries to verify their enrollment status each month, and require monthly reporting.

Improve efforts to notify veterans and schools about overpayment debts by:

- Identifying and implementing other methods of notifying veterans and schools about debts to supplement the agency's mailed notices (e.g., email, eBenefits).
- Including information on both the cause of the debt and how to repay it in debt letters.

Revise policy for calculating overpayments to increase collections by prorating tuition overpayments when veterans reduce their enrollment during the term based on the actual date of the enrollment change rather than paying additional benefits through the end of the month during which the reduction occurred.

Ensure it is recovering the full amount of tuition and fee payments if a school does not charge a veteran for any tuition or fees after dropping a class or withdrawing from school. For example, VA could adjust its overpayment calculation to account for these situations or provide schools with guidance on how to account for school refund policies when reporting enrollment and tuition changes.

AGENCY COMMENTS AND OUR EVALUATION

We provided a draft of this report to VA for review and comment and received a written response, which is reproduced in appendix II. VA agreed with each of our recommendations and identified steps it plans to take to implement them. To expand monitoring of overpayments and collections, VA plans to develop recurring reports to identify trends and areas for improvements. To address overpayments resulting from enrollment changes, VA plans to provide information on the consequences of enrollment changes in benefit letters and veteran guidance, expand outreach to schools about dual certification, and develop a system for verifying veterans' monthly enrollment. To address collection issues, VA plans to pursue additional methods of notifying veterans about overpayment debts, include information on the cause of debts and how to repay them in notification letters to schools and veterans, and adjust its regulations and procedures for prorating overpayments and accounting for school refund policies. VA also provided technical comments that we incorporated, as appropriate. We also provided selected portions of the draft to the Department of Education for review; the department did not have any comments.

Sincerely yours,
Melissa Emrey-Arras
Director, Education, Workforce, and Income Security Issues

APPENDIX I: OBJECTIVES, SCOPE, AND METHODOLOGY

The objectives of this report were to examine: (1) what is known about the extent of Post-9/11 GI Bill overpayments and collections, and how effectively the Department of Veterans Affairs' (VA) monitors them, (2) the effectiveness of VA's efforts to address the causes of overpayments, and (3) how effectively VA's policies and procedures support the collection of overpayments.

Federal Agencies, Laws, and Regulations

We reviewed relevant federal laws, regulations, Office of Management and Budget circulars, and federal standards related to financial management and the Post-9/11 GI Bill. We also reviewed documents and guidance from VA. This included claims processing and debt collection manuals, and examples of correspondence with schools and beneficiaries. We also analyzed VA's monitoring of overpayments and collections by reviewing its internal data tracking and relevant public reports, such as VA's annual Performance and Accountability Report and Quarterly High-Dollar Overpayment Reports, and assessed these efforts against guidance for government receivables in OMB Circular A-129.[1]

We interviewed senior officials from VA about the process for establishing and collecting Post-9/11 GI Bill overpayments. We also visited one of VA's four Regional Processing Offices in Muskogee, OK for interviews with management and frontline staff. We selected this location because it is co-located with VA's Education Call Center. During this site visit we met with claims processers, telephone representatives, and management to discuss the causes of overpayments and VA's actions to address them. We also visited VA's debt collection office, the Debt Management Center, which is located near St. Paul, MN. During this site visit we interviewed management and frontline staff about the various mechanisms and timelines they use to collect overpayment debts. We assessed VA's efforts to address the causes of overpayments and collect overpayment debts against the key requirements in the Post-9/11 GI Bill's statute and regulations, and government standards for internal controls. As a point of comparison, we reviewed selected documents and interviewed officials from the Department of Education about the collection policies and procedures for federal student aid programs.

Data Analysis and Case File Review

To examine the extent of overpayments and collections, we reviewed available Post-9/11 GI Bill financial data from VA. We primarily focused on overpayments that originated in fiscal years 2013 and 2014, since VA's data systems only maintain overpayment records in an accessible format for 2 years once the debts have been repaid. We reviewed summary and record level data on the frequency, type, and amount of overpayments and collections for these two fiscal years. We also analyzed data on all outstanding debts dating back to the start of the Post-9/11 GI Bill in 2009. We assessed the reliability of these data by reviewing VA's reporting systems and conducting electronic testing of the underlying data, and we determined that the data were sufficiently reliable for our reporting purposes.

To identify the causes of overpayments, we reviewed VA's Quarterly High-Dollar Overpayment Reports and supporting documentation for fiscal years 2013 and 2014 because they are VA's only source of generalizable data on overpayment causes. For these reports, VA randomly selected a sample of 251 overpayments each quarter that were over $1,667 and reviewed each claims file to identify the cause of the overpayment.[2] These samples were all drawn from overpayments for any VA education program and we estimated Post-9/11 GI Bill overpayments as a subgroup analysis, which accounted for 1,710 of the 2,008 overpayments reviewed in fiscal years 2013 and 2014. We analyzed these reports to calculate the types and frequency of issues that created overpayments and report aggregate data on high-dollar overpayments. We used methods appropriate for a stratified random sample, using weights and stratification that reflect a quarterly sample design. We convey the sampling error in the form of confidence intervals at the 95 percent confidence level. All results from a statistical sample are subject to sampling error that would result if a different randomly selected set of units from the same population had been selected. If the same sampling procedure were repeated many times, we would expect the 95 percent confidence intervals for an estimate to contain the true population value in about 95 out of 100 samples. For the last fiscal year of 2014, the number of high-dollar overpayments (the population size) was not known. We assumed it is the same as that of the previous quarter, quarter 3, and assured our estimates were not sensitive to this assumption. Specifically, we compared estimates for high-dollar amounts and overpayment causes while under three assumed scenarios for the number of high-dollar overpayments for the last quarter of fiscal year 2014: (1) the same as the previous quarter; (2) the same as the smallest observed in fiscal years 2013 and 2014; and (3) the same as the largest observed in fiscal years 2013 and 2014. Results did not substantively differ. We assessed the reliability of the data in these quarterly reports through our case file reviews and by interviewing VA officials about the processes and systems they use to develop the reports, and we determined that the data were sufficiently reliable for our reporting purposes.

We conducted an in-depth case file review of 20 overpayment cases to identify specific examples of how overpayments are created and calculated and to help assess the reliability of VA's data systems for reporting on overpayments. We selected this non-generalizable sample from the 251 cases sampled in VA's high-dollar overpayment report from the first quarter report for fiscal year 2014. From the 251 cases, we selected all four caused by VA error and randomly selected 6 of the 21 caused by school errors. We then randomly selected a sample of 10 of the 226 overpayments caused by student enrollment changes (see table 2). To review these cases, we analyzed claims processing documents, school reporting forms, and debt notification letters to determine the circumstances that created the overpayment. We also interviewed VA officials responsible for analyzing the cases for quarterly reports about the process and quality control measures.

We also examined other VA data sources for information on overpayments. For example, we reviewed available summary data and a selection of VA's school compliance surveys to identify instances of school reporting errors, reviewed a selection of 24 school compliance surveys to identify examples of school reporting errors, and reviewed veteran complaints about overpayment issues submitted through VA's GI Bill Feedback system.

Table 2. Summary Statistics from VA's FY14 1st Quarter Report on High-Dollar Overpayments

	All Education Programs	*Subset of Post-9/11 GI Bill cases*	*Number included in GAO case file review*
Sample size	251	212	
Number in sample caused by VA error	4	4	4
Number in sample caused by school error	21	21	6 (randomly selected)
Number in sample caused by student enrollment changes	226	187	10[a] (randomly selected)

Source: GAO analysis of VA's Quarter Report on High-Dollar Overpayments. GAO-16-42.

[a] After reviewing the supporting documentation, we found that 2 of the 10 cases that VA had classified as caused by student enrollment changes were actually caused by school errors. We reported these two misclassifications to VA officials who agreed with our assessment.

Interviews with Schools, Veteran Organizations, and Others

We interviewed administrators at nine institutions that enroll Post-9/11 GI Bill beneficiaries about their experiences with overpayments. We selected this nongeneralizable sample to include a mix of program lengths, sectors (public, private nonprofit, and private for-profit), schools with student veteran populations ranging from 14 to more than 14,000, and regions representing all four of VA's Regional Processing Offices, which process Post-9/11 GI Bill claims (see table 3).

We interviewed representatives from several veteran service organizations and higher education organizations to obtain their perspective on the causes and effects of overpayments. These organizations included Student Veterans of America, Iraq and Afghanistan Veterans of America, the National Association of Veterans Program Administrators, Veterans of Foreign Wars, The American Legion, American Council on Education, National Association of College and University Business Offices, and the American Association of Collegiate Registrars and Admissions Officers. We also interviewed directors from three state approving agencies—state agencies that are responsible for reviewing and approving schools for participation in VA education programs[3]—about the findings from compliance surveys they conduct to assess whether schools are adhering to applicable laws and regulations.

Table 3. Institutions Selected for Interviews with School Officials

School Name	Location	Sector	Program length	Post-9/11 GI Bill Students in FY14
George Mason University	Fairfax, VA	Public	4-year	1,647
Pratt Community College	Pratt, KS	Public	2-year	15
Red Rocks Community College	Lakewood, CO	Public	2-year	415
University of North Carolina at Asheville	Asheville, NC	Public	4-year	79
Goucher College	Baltimore, MD	Private non-profit	4-year	14
University of New Haven	West Haven, CT	Private non-profit	4-year	247
University of Southern California	Los Angeles, CA	Private non-profit	4-year	722
American Public University System	Charles Town, WV	Private for-profit	4-year	14,508
Fortis College	Smyrna, GA	Private for-profit	2-year	80

Source: GAO analysis of VA and Department of Education data. | GAO-16-42.

We conducted this performance audit from April 2014 to October 2015 in accordance with generally accepted government auditing standards. Those standards require that we plan and perform the audit to obtain sufficient, appropriate evidence to provide a reasonable basis for our findings and conclusions based on our audit objectives. We believe that the evidence obtained provides a reasonable basis for our findings and conclusions based on our audit objectives.

End Notes

1 In this report we generally refer to Post-9/11 GI Bill beneficiaries as veterans, although under certain circumstances, veterans can transfer their Post-9/11 GI Bill benefits to their spouses and children. 38 U.S.C. § 3319.

2 OMB Circular A-129 provides guidance to agencies for, among other things, managing the federal government's receivables (also referred to as claims or debts), including

overpayments to beneficiaries. Executive Office of the President, OMB Circular A-129 (as revised Jan. 2013).

[3] Post-9/11 Veterans Educational Assistance Act of 2008, Pub. L. No. 110-252, tit. V, § 5003(d), 122 Stat. 2357, 2378.

[4] 38 U.S.C. § 3311(b)(8).

[5] 38 U.S.C. §§ 3311(b)(1) and 3313(c)(1). Veterans can also receive full benefits if they served on active duty for at least 30 continuous days and where discharged due to service-connected disability. Veterans who served on active duty for less than 36 months are eligible for a portion of the maximum tuition amount based on their time served. Veterans attending participating nonprofit or for-profit schools may receive additional benefits to cover tuition and fees through the Yellow Ribbon G.I. Education Enhancement Program (Yellow Ribbon Program). 38 U.S.C. § 3317. Through this program, schools enter into voluntary agreements with VA to pay a portion of the tuition and fees that exceed an individual's Post-9/11 GI Bill benefit and VA matches the schools' contribution.

[6] 38 U.S.C. § 3313(h).

[7] 38 U.S.C. § 3313(c)(1)(B)(i)-(iii). The monthly housing allowance is based on the Department of Defense Basic Allowance for Housing. Students enrolled exclusively online can also receive a portion of the housing allowance.

[8] 38 C.F.R. § 21.9720.

[9] However, overpayments caused by school reporting or VA processing errors are counted as improper payments. An improper payment is defined by statute as any payment that should not have been made or that was made in an incorrect amount (including overpayments and underpayments) under statutory, contractual, administrative, or other legally applicable requirements. 31 U.S.C. § 3321 note. It includes, for example, any payment to an ineligible recipient, any payment for an ineligible good or service, any duplicate payment, and any payment for a good or service not received (except for such payments where authorized by law).

[10] Veterans must also repay benefits for any courses in which they received a grade that does not earn credit towards their degree (e.g., incomplete, no credit).

[11] 38 U.S.C. § 3685.

[12] 38 C.F.R. § 21.9695(b)(2).

[13] Schools are also responsible if the overpayment is the result of willful or negligent (1) false certification by a school or (2) failure by a school to certify excessive absences, discontinuance of a course by the school, or interruption of a course by the veteran. 38 C.F.R. § 21.9695(b)(3).

[14] 38 C.F.R. § 21.9695(b)(1)(ii).

[15] 38 U.S.C. § 5302(a) and 38 C.F.R. § 1.963. The standard for granting a waiver is that recovery would be "against equity and good conscience." VA officials also noted that only veterans have the option of requesting a waiver; schools may not do so. Veterans also have the option of submitting a compromise offer (of a lesser amount) to settle a debt, but officials from VA's Debt Management Center said they have not accepted any compromise offers for Post-9/11 GI Bill debts.

[16] GAO, Veterans' Education Benefits: Enhanced Guidance and Collaboration Could Improve Administration of the Post-9/11 GI Bill Program, GAO-11-356R (Washington, D.C.: May 5, 2011).

[17] Schools can only receive tuition and fee overpayments, while veterans can receive overpayments for tuition, housing, and books.

[18] VA is required to produce quarterly reports on high-dollar overpayments. Exec. Order No. 13,520, § 3(f), 74 Fed. Reg. 62,201, 62,203 (Nov. 20, 2009). For fiscal years 2013 and 2014, VA reviewed a sample of overpayments each quarter that were over $1,667.

[19] Similarly, enrollment changes account for the vast majority of overpayment dollars. For example, we estimated that veteran enrollment changes account for around $247 million of the $280 million high-dollar overpayments VA made in fiscal year 2014. VA's estimate of 90 percent is based on a sample with a 95 percent confidence level and a ± 5 percent confidence interval. Our dollar estimates are based on a sample with 95 percent confidence intervals of $226 million to $267 million for student enrollment changes and $259 million to $301 million for the total.

[20] Overpayments were distributed among the different types of schools that enroll veterans. In fiscal year 2014, for-profit schools received $70 million in overpayments (94 percent of which had been repaid to VA by November 2014), public schools had received $44 million (95 percent of which had been repaid by November 2014), and nonprofit schools had received $32 million (96 percent of which had been repaid by November 2014).

[21] These collection rates also reflect the flexibility that VA offers to veterans to enter into repayment plans for their overpayment debts, which can generally last up to a year.

[22] In fiscal year 2014, VA collected 61 percent of veteran overpayments by deducting the debts from subsequent GI Bill or other VA payments, 23 percent from direct payments, 12 percent from offsetting other federal payments, and 5 percent from private debt collection agencies. Percentages do not sum to 100 due to rounding.

[23] VA's payment and collections data systems are continuously updated and reconciled as overpayments occur and are collected; however, VA management does not actively monitor this information.

[24] The Improper Payments Information Act of 2002 requires executive agencies to determine whether any of their programs are susceptible to significant improper payment and annually report estimates of improper payments for any such programs. Pub. L. No. 107-300, § 2(d)(2), 116 Stat. 2350, 2350-51 (codified as amended at 31 U.S.C. § 3321 note). The act defines an improper payment as any payment that should not have been made or that was made in an incorrect amount (including overpayments and underpayments) under statutory, contractual, administrative, or other legally applicable requirements. This includes, for example, any payment to an ineligible recipient, any payment for an ineligible good or service, any duplicate payment, and any payment for a good or service not received (except for such payments where authorized by law).

[25] While VA collects some information on overpayments caused by enrollment changes for its Quarterly High-Dollar Overpayment Reports, these reports are primarily focused on improper payments.

[26] The Debt Management Center's annual report also provides aggregate information on total collections for multiple VA benefit programs, but not program-specific information, although the types of debts and populations served by each program are significantly different (e.g., students using the Post-9/11 GI Bill vs. homebuyers using the Home Loan program).

[27] Exec. Office of the President, OMB Circular A-129, § IV.A.2 (Jan. 2013).

[28] 38 C.F.R. § 21.4254(b)(9). This requirement generally affects schools that are not already subject to the Department of Education's requirement to disclose their institutional refund policies. 34 C.F.R. § 668.43(a)(2).

[29] VA calculates tuition and housing overpayments by prorating the student's attendance based on the portion of the class attended, rounded up to the end of that month the student dropped the class.

[30] VA launched its GI Bill Feedback System in January 2014 to accept complaints about schools from veterans using the GI Bill.

[31] GAO, Standards for Internal Control in the Federal Government, GAO/AIMD-00-21.3.1 (Washington, D.C.: Nov. 1, 1999).

[32] National Association of College and University Business Officers, Student Financial Services Policies and Procedures (Washington, D.C.: March 2015).

[33] The other two schools waited to submit any enrollment information to VA until about 1 week after their terms begin, which avoids some overpayments from enrollment changes but may delay housing payments to veterans.

[34] GAO/AIMD-00-21.3.1.

[35] Students who receive education benefits through VA for traditional degree and certificate programs (such as those under the Montgomery GI Bill–Active Duty, Montgomery GI Bill–Selected Reserve, and the Reserve Educational Assistance Program), as well as for on-the job-training, apprenticeships, or correspondence training programs are generally required to verify their enrollment monthly. 38 C.F.R. §§ 21.4203 and 21.4204.

[36] While delays in reporting enrollment changes can create larger housing overpayments, they do not affect the amount of tuition overpayments. This is because tuition is a onetime charge paid up front and the amount of the overpayment is based on the date the veteran dropped the class, rather than when the enrollment change was reported.

[37] VA officials said the current enrollment verification system used for other GI Bill programs is not compatible with the Post-9/11 GI Bill's data systems.

[38] 31 U.S.C. § 3512(c) and GAO/AIMD-00-21.3.1.

[39] GAO/AIMD-00-21.3.1.

[40] School officials also make data entry errors. In addition, VA's high-dollar overpayment reports also classify as school errors any overpayments resulting from changes schools report to correct tuition and fee information. For example, schools may need to revise the tuition amount after a student receives a scholarship or adjust certain fees, such as health insurance premiums. VA's estimate of 8 percent is based on a sample with a 95 percent confidence level and a ± 5 percent confidence interval. Our dollar estimates are based on a sample with 95 percent confidence intervals of $19 million to $36 million for school errors and $259 million to $301 million for the total.

[41] Department of Veterans Affairs, Office of Inspector General, Audit of Post-9/11 G.I. Bill Monthly Housing Allowance and Book Stipend Payments, 13-01452-214 (Washington, D.C.: July 11, 2014).

[42] VA also hosts quarterly webinars to provide updates and answer questions, participates in education conferences sponsored by other organizations, and school officials can request advice via VA's school official hotline or their VA education liaisons. Additionally, compliance survey officials can provide some targeted training during compliance reviews.

[43] In 2011, for example, VA implemented our recommendation to raise awareness of training opportunities for school certifying officials by creating a central website for information about online training and conferences. See GAO, VA Education Benefits: Actions Taken, but Outreach and Oversight Could Be Improved, GAO-11-256 (Washington, D.C.: Feb. 28, 2011). More recently in 2014, the VA Inspector General recommended that the agency reinforce the need for school certifying officials to complete the agency's training, which VA has since implemented by sending school certifying officials an email to remind them

of available online training and highlighting training resources for school certifying officials during an August 2014 webinar. See Department of Veterans Affairs, 13-01452-214.

[44] GAO/AIMD-00-21.3.1.

[45] VA's estimate of 2 percent is based on a sample with a 95 percent confidence level and a ± 5 percent confidence interval. Our dollar estimates are based on a sample with 95 percent confidence intervals of $3 million to $10 million for VA errors and $259 million to $301 million for the total.

[46] 38 U.S.C. § 3313(c)(1)(B)(i).

[47] VA officials said veterans generally have to contact VA's Education Call Center to update their address. Any address changes submitted to other VA programs are not uploaded into the veteran's Post-9/11 GI Bill records. Even address changes submitted through VA's eBenefits website are not always automatically uploaded into the Post-9/11 GI Bill system. For returned mail, officials from the Debt Management Center said they try to identify correct addresses through various address search providers. School addresses are continually updated in VA's school directory database.

[48] 38 C.F.R. § 3.103. The mailed notification letters also include essential information on veterans' other due process rights, such as the opportunity to request an oral hearing or seek representation from a veteran service organization or attorney.

[49] 31 U.S.C. § 3711(e)(1)(C) and 38 C.F.R. § 1.911(b).

[50] GAO/AIMD-00-21.3.1

[51] VA also sends schools a monthly summary of any outstanding overpayment debts. School administrators we spoke with said this summary is beneficial because it helps them better track their debts. However, a few school administrators said they would still prefer a means to obtain real-time information on their debts.

[52] As for schools, VA officials said that its Stakeholder Enterprise Portal, which is currently designed as a tool for veteran service organizations, could potentially be expanded for use as a portal for communications with schools. The agency does not currently have any plans to implement this upgrade.

[53] 38 C.F.R. § 1.911(b) and (c).

[54] According to the law, VA is authorized to prorate overpayment debts based on the student's period of enrollment if the student is ordered to active duty or if the student can document that mitigating circumstances—unanticipated and unavoidable events beyond a student's control (e.g., illness or injury, change in employment)—are responsible for the student's inability to complete a course. 38 U.S.C. § 3680(a)(3). However, VA's current practice is to prorate all overpayment debts whether or not the student meets these criteria, according to VA officials.

[55] 38 U.S.C. § 3680(a).

[56] When a veteran withdraws from some but not all of their classes, VA's overpayment calculation would instead prorate the overpayment amount as though the veteran had kept attending class through the end of the month rather than using the actual date of the withdrawal, as previously discussed.

[57] These three schools included one from each sector: public, private nonprofit, and private for-profit.

[58] 38 U.S.C. § 3313(c)(1).

End Notes for Appendix I

[1] Exec. Office of the President, Policies for Federal Credit Programs and Non-Tax Receivables, OMB Circular A-129 (as revised Jan. 2013).

[2] VA is required to produce quarterly reports on high-dollar overpayments. Exec. Order No. 13,520, § 3(f), 74 Fed. Reg. 62,201, 62,203 (Nov. 20, 2009).

[3] 38 U.S.C. § 3313(b).

INDEX

P

R

S

T

U

W